Slick Watts's

TALES FROM THE

SEATTLE SUPERSONICS

SLICK WATTS
WITH
FRANK HUGHES

FOREWORD BY
JACK SIKMA

www.SportsPublishingLLC.com

ISBN: 1-58261-904-2

Publishers: Peter L. Bannon and Joseph J. Bannon Sr.
Senior managing editor: Susan M. Moyer
Acquisitions editor: Bob Snodgrass
Developmental editor: Travis W. Moran
Art director: K. Jeffrey Higgerson
Dust jacket design and imaging: Heidi Norsen
Project manager: Greg Hickman
Photo editor: Erin Linden-Levy
Media and promotions managers: Kelley Brown (regional),
    Randy Fouts (national), Maurey Williamson (print)

Printed in the United States of America

Sports Publishing L.L.C.
804 North Neil Street
Champaign, IL 61820

Phone: 1-877-424-2665
Fax: 217-363-2073
Web: www.SportsPublishingLLC.com

For my family.

—Slick Watts

For my wife, Wendy, and our three sons.

—Frank Hughes

Contents

ACKNOWLEDGMENTS

I'd like to thank everybody who made this book possible. My wife and my family, the NBA family past and present, especially the Seattle SuperSonics and my teammates. I'd also like to thank the fans for their support and inspiration throughout my life.

—Slick Watts

FOREWORD

There are many great stories about what's happened with the Sonics franchise—from the early days to now—for the loyal fan base that started with the team from the beginning. I remember coming to Seattle for the first time and thinking that there was quite a connection between the fans and the players. Seattle was still a small town back then. Both the town and the team have evolved into this huge thing, but there still are the people who come up and talk about the early days.

I think there is no better person to tell some of the stories than Slick Watts. Slick is just a fantastic guy. He was a key marketing tool for the organization. He was one of the primary reasons that people were coming to the games in the '70s. He just really put the Sonics on the map. He broadened the base from the hardcore fans who were there from the beginning to the more established entity that is there now.

When I was drafted with the No. 8 pick out of Illinois Wesleyan, the only thing I knew about Seattle was Slick. I had read a *Sports Illustrated* story about Bill Russell and Slick. But I had never been to Seattle; knew nothing about Seattle. Actually, I played in a senior college all-star game in Tulsa, Oklahoma, and then another in Hawaii. That was the first time I had been west of the Rockies.

Slick was "The Man" when I got here. In training camp, he took Joe Hassett, another rookie, and me out to dinner, told us how things were. He was very gracious.

I remember him as being very confident in his abilities. Slick and I had a good thing going at practice too, because he always penetrated, and I was a pretty good defensive center, so we often met in the middle. It never got feisty or heated. It wasn't about being feisty. It was about playing hard and getting better. We were teammates. I wasn't competing for Slick's job or he for my job.

Even after Slick was traded away, he has stayed connected to the team and Seattle—and he is the perfect fit for this type of book. It is going to be fun to read with Slick's personality because he is gregarious and open. We all feel connected with Slick. Anyone that follows Sonics history and follows Slick knows how funny and entertaining he is.

He is that way now and was that way when I first arrived in Seattle, which was something of a controversial occurrence. Although I was the eighth pick in the draft, there were still some other players—Ernie Grunfeld, Tom LaGarde, Ray Williams, "Cornbread" Maxwell—out there. I think it really came down to Bob Hopkins. He really wanted me. He was willing to step out and take me.

I remember Lenny Wilkens calling my college coach and telling him that if I were available they were going to take me. And I had heard from Portland and the Lakers, but they were drafting down in the teens. So I was thinking, "The eighth pick in the draft?" I was pretty excited about it. And then I started to think, "Maybe they meant, 'if you were available in the second round.'"

I remember my first game in the summer league was down in L.A. against Moses Malone. Moses killed me. Sam Schulman, the Sonics owner who lived in L.A., was there, and he went up to Les Habegger, an assistant coach, and asked, "Is *this* our first-round pick?"

I remember I started my first game in the 22nd game of the year. We were on a four-game road trip. We had just lost to Denver and were on the way to Kansas City. I was walking down the hall after that game and ran into Hoppy, and he said, "Hey Jack, they let me go." They had fired my first coach.

Then there was a meeting with Lenny, who took over for Hoppy. "We have this team," he said, "we are confident in you, and we are going to play the rest of the season like this."

I remember I had a bonus in my contract; if I started 15 games, I got a bonus. The next game, Lenny didn't start me. So I had earned the starting job under one coach, and he got fired, and the next game I didn't start. I thought I was going to lose my bonus. As it turned out, the season turned around, and I did get my bonus—and more.

We won the last three games of that road trip, started playing well, and by the holidays, we were close to .500, and there was talk we were going to make a run of it. Did we ever—we ran all the way to the NBA Finals.

I knew I was part of something special, but I didn't know how special it was going to be. When you think about how fast we came together, the rest of my career really never rivaled that period. We were young, and it was emotional. We were playing an exciting brand of basketball. We got it rolling. There was intensity to the whole season, and we really played hard. We just got pushed along.

We lost to the Washington Bullets in seven games in the Finals that season. But that year carried over to the next year, and we won the first and only professional men's championship in the city's history.

From the oldest fan to the youngest fans on Seattle streets, everywhere you went was a celebration. When you look back, you could just tell that there was tremendous excitement.

Seattle is a unique sports town because of its allegiance to Husky football. Their co-national championship will be remembered always, as will the year the Mariners won 116 games.

But Seattle will always be connected to that 1979 championship team—even after we all die away.

—Jack Sikma

Chapter 1

Humble Beginnings

Because Seattle is a relatively young town, and because the SuperSonics were the city's first professional sports franchise (instituted in 1967), the Sonics will always hold a special place in the heart of the Emerald City.

In a town that embraces whichever team is successful, that's not to say that the Sonics are always the most popular. But it suggests that, no matter what else is happening, the Sonics will always possess an exclusive standing by simple virtue of their place in the city's sporting lore (they remain the only professional men's team to win a championship—the Seattle Storm won a title in 2004).

I came along in the team's seventh season, and I became the city's first sports icon, its first superstar. It happened not necessarily because of my physical talent. After all, I was an undrafted free agent out of Xavier University in Louisiana, and I was only six foot one and 175 pounds.

Certainly, Spencer Haywood, who tore down backboards in the Olympics, was more talented, and the great Bill Russell, my coach, had accomplished more. But those men were so big, they

Slick gives a young fan a lift.
From the Donald Watts Collection

were almost untouchable—like gods. People were too intimidated to even approach them—which is how Russell liked it.

I was a man of the people—a player for the people. I was a fighter, a scratcher, a biter, a hatchet. My best skill was my quickness, and I got the most out of it—darting back and forth on defense, diving on the floor for balls, upsetting the tempo of the game.

People loved that; they loved to see an underdog-type player get the maximum out of his ability. They appreciated what I was able to accomplish with the limited skills I had. So in a city without a sports hero to worship, I was—out of pure circumstance—in the right place at the right time.

It didn't hurt that I had some unique characteristics: the bald head, the headband, and, of course, the nickname.

It may seem ridiculous now—especially after Michael Jordan made it such a fashionable look—but in the '70s being bald wasn't cool. Big afros—made stylish by James Brown—were in. You only walked around bald because you had lost your hair. Certainly, nobody like me, in his early twenties, intentionally walked around bald. But I did, and I was proud of it. Also, nobody really wore headbands. Wilt Chamberlain wore a yellow one, but few other players did. I wore it stylishly, sometimes tilted to the left, sometimes to the right, sometimes straight, and people loved it.

Of course, having a nickname like Slick never hurts. To this day, my wife calls me Don, and my mama calls me Donald Earl. But everybody else calls me Slick. Those traits made me recognizable but also made me approachable. While Spencer and Russell were larger than life, I was somebody the fans could talk to, could relate to, somebody with whom they could identify.

And I could identify with them because I came into the NBA as a fan more than I did as a player. I played with and against some of the best players in the history of the game, and I mean it when I say I, a little ol' boy from Mississippi, am in awe of that.

It was an honor to play against Wilt and Pistol Pete Maravich and Kareem Abdul-Jabbar and Jerry West and Oscar Robertson.

I would call home and tell my family about it. Somehow I don't think those players were calling home to tell their mamas they played against Slick Watts.

But it was that approach to my profession, and my congenial personality, that endeared me to Seattle perhaps more than anyone before or since.

As Sean Spain said in *What's Up* Magazine about the Bellingham, Washington band that named itself after me: "They rock hard but with a wink and a smile instead of an attitude." That accurately describes the band Slick Watts and the person Slick Watts.

My celebrity allowed me to become good friends with Bob Lanier, Moses Malone, Reggie Jackson, Jesse Jackson, and many others. It allowed me to meet President Jimmy Carter, Muhammad Ali, The Jackson Five, and Lola Falana. I was one of the few people to have close relationships with both Russell and Chamberlain at a time when the media portrayed them as mortal enemies.

I had the opportunity to be coached by Elgin Baylor, Lenny Wilkens, and of course, Russell. I played with Rick Barry, Calvin Murphy, Spencer Haywood, Fred Brown, Jack Sikma, Maravich, and Malone. These are some self-assured men. Those experiences gave me some insight to big, powerful personalities.

My superstardom didn't last long. It happened quickly, rather unexpectedly, like a shooting star. And it ended in Seattle four and a half years later as I became a victim of my own success. But when I was rolling, when I was clicking, it was the greatest time of my life.

It has been said that if I had run for governor of Washington state back then, I would have won. I was named the SeaFair Grand Marshall twice. I had a song written about me by country singer Jim Tate called, "Slick is his name, let him play his game." I had to move twice because people were camped outside my house in Kirkland. I was on billboards, on the sides of buses, on the news every night. To be honest, I got sick and tired of seeing myself everywhere. I really did.

In a way, though, that celebrity lives on, and that's why I continue to live in Seattle. Though they'd probably never admit it, I suspect that's why so many former Sonics players and coaches from my era—Russell, Lenny Wilkens, Fred Brown, John Johnson, Jack Sikma, Talvin Skinner, Dean Tolson, Bob Hopkins—continue to live in the Seattle area and have an affiliation with the team.

I love walking into a Safeway or a QFC and having fans recognize me and come up to have a 10-minute conversation. I love doing speaking engagements with kids. I was a part of one of the greatest periods of this organization's history—the tenure of Bill Russell and the years leading up to the 1978-79 championship. Those memories help define who I am today, and they will never fade.

I will share most of those memories with you in this book, but first I want to give a deeper understanding of the three things that made me distinctive at the time.

THE HAIR

When I was in middle school—about 13 years old—I played football. Back then, they used to teach you how to tackle wrong, with your head down. So, of course, I was trying to impress the coach and I made a tackle. I had been unconscious, and when I got up, I was bleeding from my head. I had damaged a nerve in the back of my head. In fact, I still have the mark where I was injured.

When I went to the hospital, they shaved my head. And for some reason, my hair started growing back in uneven patches all over my head. The kids used to call me "Map Head." You know, like when you look at a map and you see Texas and Mississippi in different shapes and shades of color.

Those were the days when The Beatles had their hair down and James Brown and all the brothers wore afros. And here I was with a shaved head. It wasn't as cool as it is now, but my Daddy told me my hair looked better all the way off than like a map. So I shaved it because I was trying to get away from being ridiculed and teased every day.

When I shaved it, I locked myself in the gym every day. Every day. I didn't have any friends, because shaving your head wasn't the cool thing. Nobody wanted to be around the freak.

So I hooped—it was my escape from reality. That was a big issue in my life, accepting that I was different.

THE HEADBAND

It actually started by luck. People thought I did it as a fashion statement or that I was trying to be different or whatever, but it was luck. I appreciate that now, because it has grown to be such a huge part of who I am.

I played ball in college, and because I was bald and I sweated so much, water used to run everywhere. I said, "I have to find a way to keep this water off me." So, I took a piece of white tape and I actually taped it on my head. After the game, the trainer almost had to cut it off my head.

I thought, "Oh, this tape thing isn't going to work."

So I looked around and I found one headband—a black one. I think I found the only one in the whole world. Nobody was wearing them. I think Wilt Chamberlain was wearing a gold one. I put on that headband, and I kept that headband three years in college. Every quarter I would go to the sideline and wring it out and put it back on. Every year I wore it, and everybody wanted to come see the freak. It was like the greatest show on earth when we came to a school. They were waiting to see me, and they would call me a freak.

The world wasn't as open and accepting as it is now.

Headband like a ring of Saturn.
From the Donald Watts Collection

I wore it three different ways. When I was shooting well, I would put it back straight. If I tilt it, I had a tendency to shoot it whichever way I tilt it. I had a philosophy that if I started it over to the right, and I was shooting the ball right, I would bring it back to the left. If I was shooting left, I would bring it back to center. If I started it right, and I was going good, I wouldn't mess with it. So I kind of played with it, but I had a little more style when I cocked it a little bit.

I got to the point where I started getting famous, and I kind of wanted to distance myself from the image. So one day I tried to not wear it.

Russ looked at me and said, "Get your ass back in there and get that headband."

So I went and got it. I figured it was a part of me if the Big Fella made me put it back on.

Former Sonics announcer Bob Blackburn remembers another angle on the headbands:

"Slick knows what show business is all about," Blackburn said. "And basketball is show business just like anything else. Consequently, that was why he was such a lovely character, the way he would give sweatbands to the girls after the game. He always had a good supply around. If there were pretty girls, he always made sure they got a headband."

THE NAME

Sister Mary Francis from Xavier University gave me the name. They used to call me "Shine." Then they called me "Head." They also used to call me "Eagle," as in "Bald Eagle."

But one night, we were playing Grambling, and I had 12 steals. The next day before class, Sister Mary Francis said, "You are so slick."

Then, as kids were coming to class, she said, "Did you see that Watts boy? He just played so slick."

As we played the next night, the cheerleaders started chanting: "Deal Slick, Deal. Deal Slick, Deal."

And it just caught on like fire.

CHAPTER 2

WELCOME TO THE NBA

The year I came into the NBA was also the year that Bill Russell—winner of 11 championships in 13 years with the Boston Celtics—began his short-lived and rather controversial coaching career.

Russell was brought in for two reasons. First, because of his name. As Sonics owner Sam Schulman proved a few years earlier with Spencer Haywood, who took the league all the way to the Supreme Court in an effort to be able to play professionally without having attended three years of college, Schulman was not afraid to try the spectacular. Having the winningest player in the history of the league coach your team certainly qualified as spectacular.

But Russell also was supposed to rein in a group of players who had migrated to the NBA from the ABA. Spencer, John Brisker, and Jim McDaniels were the first of their group to earn the so-called million-dollar contracts. However, while their egos were big enough to match their contracts, Russell's ego was even bigger.

Schulman was spending a ton of money on those three players, and yet they had failed to produce the way he had envisioned. Russell's task was to either find a way to make those three players successful or find a way to run some or all out of town so that Schulman no longer had to pay their hefty contracts.

Russell was intimidated by no man, and in fact took pleasure in using his daunting, seven-foot frame to impose his will on people. No matter what a player was making, Russell was going to make that player bow down to him. Schulman may have been giving out big contracts, but he was going to make sure that Russell kept the players who were earning them—or not earning them, as the case may be—in line.

Of course, I didn't know any of this when I finished my senior season at Xavier. In fact, as I soon found out, there was a great deal about the NBA—and life for that matter—that I didn't know.

SLICK, FRESH, AND GREEN

When the NBA draft came around, I thought I was going to get drafted. I was sitting down there at the *New Orleans Times-Picayune*, waiting for the phone to ring. Bill Fitch, who was coaching Cleveland at the time, told me he was going to draft me. I thought because my name began with "W" that I was going to be drafted by alphabet. I thought they drafted alphabetically. I didn't know they drafted who they wanted based on skill. So as the rounds passed, and I didn't get drafted, I said, "Well, W is coming up. I should be next."

But it never happened.

My coach at Xavier, Bob Hopkins, played four years in the NBA with Syracuse, and Bill Russell was his cousin. I was completely shocked when I wasn't drafted. So Hopkins called Bill Russell.

*Bob Hopkins (center) with Slick and
three teammates from Xavier.*
From the Donald Watts Collection

I was sitting there in the training room at Xavier, and Hopkins said to Russ, "We got a little kid here, he plays with a lot of heart, he plays great defense, he's not afraid to stick his nose in there."

That's the thing that really impressed me, to have the opportunity to even talk to Russell on the phone. I was intimidated, more or less, just by his voice. I think he knew that just by the way he talked down to you.

So Bill Russell said, "Let me talk to the boy."

So I got on the phone, and he said in his big deep voice, "Boy, I heard you can play."

I said, "Yes, sir, I can play."

He said, "How tall are you?"

I said, "Six foot one."

And he said, "That's mighty small."

I said, "But I got long arms."

He said, "But can you play?"

I think the one that did it—the one that got him on my side—was when I said, "Can you coach? If you can coach, I can play."

"Boy, you got a big mouth," he shot back. "Let me speak to Coach Hopkins."

Hopkins got on the phone, and Russell said, "Get the boy on the plane and get him up here."

I guess nobody had ever said something like that to him.

IS SEATTLE ON THE EAST COAST?

That summer I sold all of my furniture, paid all my bills off, and got my plane ticket. I had one little bag, slippers, and a big old hat. At first I thought I was going to Washington, D.C. I didn't have an understanding of the map or geography at that time. I didn't even think about Seattle.

Down south, we didn't relate to Seattle. All I knew was the Pacific Ocean. We talked about California; we talked about San Francisco, but Seattle was a place that wasn't even on your mind. Plus, they didn't have a team until '68-69.

At the time, I hadn't even been to Chicago. I said, "I'm going to be where the president is at."

I got on the plane thinking I was going to Washington, D.C. I then heard the captain say, "You are now landing in Denver," (because we had a connection to Seattle).

I remember thinking, "I thought I was going to the East Coast."

WELCOME, WE'RE GLAD YOU'RE HERE

Russell's personality was so big, he didn't even bother coming over to talk to the rookies. We were all staying at a hotel on Sixth Avenue, and for some reason, we had a team meeting in my room. We had all these seven-footers from the big schools. I had never seen so many big people together in my life. We were in my room, and you couldn't even see me with all these big people.

Russell had sent over Emmette Bryant, who had played for a year with Russ in Boston and who was now an assistant coach. We called him, "Em."

Em greeted us, saying, "Personally, I don't even know what you all are doing here, because I have 12 contracts already. I guess the team needed a tax write-off." He was just putting fear in us young rookies, intimidating us, just raining on our dream.

"If you make it," he says, "it's a miracle. I have 12 guys already and no cuts. Maybe I can find one or two guys who can help us."

I called my daddy after the meeting and told him, "I think I'm coming home."

"No," he said, "you hang in there and play."

ROOKIE CAMP

Back then, we had rookie camp for five days before we had the real training camp to decide which rookies were going to make it to training camp. Rookie camp was at Seattle Pacific University.

Everybody could really play. You might think that you would go to veteran camp because of the higher skill level. But you go to rookie camp, because that is where everybody is hungry.

Nothing on their table, baby. Players pick you up full court. Players elbow you in your head and your jock. Those players hate you.

So Russell started rookie training camp for five days, and every day I had a slipped disc in my back, and I couldn't really touch my toes.

In college, I used to carry a pillow with me to hide the fact that I had a slipped disk in my back. "Soft Booty" is what they called me because they knew I needed that pillow. But I couldn't sit down without it. When I got on planes or buses, after we took off I actually laid underneath the seat in the back of the plane.

I don't know how I overcame that injury. My back was always killing me. Then at 25 or 26 years old, the injury just left me. I'm one of those guys who doesn't believe in getting sliced anyway. No surgery for me, that's for sure. I once had a torn meniscus, and I healed that myself with ice.

But when I had that pillow they used to say, "There goes Soft Booty." But I could handle anything. After going through that "Map Head" trauma, nothing bothered me. That's why I could play on the road. I had gone through a lot of ridicule in my life, so nothing really got me down. That's where I am now: I will answer to anything.

People ask me, "What should I call you, Slick or Don?"

I say, "Whatever comes out your mouth, I'm all right with it."

Anyway, in rookie camp, I couldn't really touch my toes. But when Bill Russell came in that gym and said, "Toe touches," I would go all the way down. Back in those days, there were no bonus babies, not like today's rookies. If you were damaged goods, you were out—so you didn't let people know you were injured.

Every night, I would have a little kid come over and help me pull off my shoes and socks. Then I would take an ice bath. That was hard to do. I would just lay there. I had a string and I would keep my privates out of the ice and just soak my back.

BAD DAY FOR RUSS

Em Bryant would run rookie practice, and Russell would come in with his bat over his shoulder, cackling, and start talking about particular players. "Look how funny he looks." He would talk about you like a dog. "You can't play no basketball, boy, look at you."

Then one day he came in just pissed off. I think he must have shot a bad round of golf or something. He came in and there were about 12 guys on the floor, and he said, "Get them all out of here, get 'em out."

He sent everybody home. I think he had already made up his mind who he was going to cut, but he planned everything out in his mind. Like in the movies, he was really good at playing with your psyche. I think Red Auerbach got him into that. When he told everybody to get out, it instilled so much fear in the rookies.

All of us felt, "no man is God;" but as far as we were concerned, Russ was a big, six-foot-11, black god.

Well . . . either God or the Devil.

GETTING CUT—OR SO I THOUGHT

At the end of rookie camp, Russell came into the dressing room after the rookie scrimmage. I had 15 points in that scrimmage and played pretty well. Still, everyone was sitting on the bench with their heads down. Russ looked us over and said, "If I call your name, go in the other room."

He was twisting it around, because at first if he called your name it meant go home. But this time he said, "If I call your name, go in the other room." We didn't know if it meant go home or stay or what. He was always in your head—always in your head.

So Em starts calling out names. "Harold Fox." Harold thinks he's gone.

"Larry Hollyfield," a guy from UCLA. He broke down. "I know I can play. I know I can play." He broke down hard. We all thought he had died. Russell was cackling.

"Slick Watts."

I thought, "I'm cut."

William Harris, the big boy from North Carolina A&T, was the other to be called. We all went in and sat down. I thought they were coming to tell us to get the hell out. To this day, I don't know what they told the other guys.

As we were saying goodbye to each other, Russell came over and said, "Guys, go back to the hotel and get your stuff, you're going to Port Angeles with us." Port Angeles was where they held training camp. I couldn't believe it. My emotions just changed from hurricane to sunshine.

We didn't see the other guys again.

MAKING IT—BUT NOT REALLY

My first year in the league was the beginning of the million-dollar players. Spencer had signed a six-year, $1.5 million deal, which at the time was big money. So, like a dummy, before we went to training camp in Port Angeles, I walked into Russell's office and said, "Coach, what about my contract?"

Russ just looked at me and said, "Boy, let me see what you can do against the big boys."

GOING TO THE MOVIES

Before we went to Port Angeles, over on the Peninsula, we were meeting down on Harrison Street, where the office used to be, and we had a big ol' bus to take us over to Port Angeles.

I will never forget this: we rookies got on the bus first. Dick Snyder and Spencer Haywood and all these guys came rolling up one at a time in their Mercedes. They weren't like Gary Payton—they didn't have nine or 10 people with them—but they did have one or two.

They had hot women—real hot women—with them.

We rookies were sitting on the bus, looking through the window at these guys who were all-pros and first-round draft picks—driving up in their Benzes with all their ladies, and we were sitting there like little children in a candy store—it was like a movie.

They all had their timing. Spencer was last and, when he came up, he had a big ol' green Cadillac. He was the man: his head was that big, and Russell's head was even bigger. Fred Brown came driving up, and he had the big ol' afro, a gigantic afro. John Brisker boarded, and he was real smooth and cool. He had an ivory cream Mercedes. He was real smooth—a physique like he could do anything, shoulders all straight. He was letting you know, "I'm the man, don't mess with me." He got on the bus, and everybody was quiet.

That was a trip, just watching everybody line up and get on the bus. And I said to myself, "Oh, so this is how the pros do it."

The Man—Russell—he drove over by himself. He always kept it different.

MEETING THE GREATEST
RUNNING BACK EVER

Jim Brown came down to camp the second or third day. I think Jim and Bill were good friends from being the best in their respective sports. Jim was a little different from Bill; Jim was cool—really cool. Russ was cool, but Russ always had so much stuff with him—he always wanted you to know that he was king.

Jim talked to you, made you feel good about yourself. He came in and said, "Yo, Watts, yo, Slick, you got game, man."

That was a big statement coming from Jim. I felt like God had just talked to me. God I was my coach, and God II was Jim Brown. Good ol' boy from Mississippi gets a chance to meet Jim Brown, after all those times I had seen him run through the Green Bay Packers line, I was really impressed to be able to meet him. That was a highlight of my life, meeting him.

He was there until the end of camp. We had a little game and Jim was sitting on the bench with us. He just watched practice—sometimes he would get out there and run the weave with us.

I guess he had a little game.

TRAINING CAMP

I played better against the veterans than I did against the rookies. One day, I lit it up. Every team I was on, we won.

Russell called me over and said, "Boy, you know what the f--- you are doing out there?"

"Coach, what did I tell you?" I said. "I told you: If you can coach, I can play."

"Get the f--- away from me," he said.

Russell was moody, which scared me a little. You could never get comfortable with him. You could never get to that position where you could say, "Coach likes me," because you never knew where he was going. Still, I called home and told Mama, "I think I'm going to make it."

GETTING MY FIRST CONTRACT

One day during practice, Russell said, "Come here, boy. Sit down." I was really scared now.

"You are f---ing up my practice."

"I'm just playing, coach, and working hard."

He says, "I can't get no plays called with you out there."

I thought I was in trouble—but he was talking about my defense. I was stealing the ball too often in the scrimmages.

About the third day of camp, he called me into his office and said, "Boy, sign this."

So I signed it—no lawyer, no representative, nothing—$1,500 as a signing bonus, $23,000 for the year. And like a dummy, I went to the post office in Port Angeles, took about $1,400 out and mailed it to my mama. I was sure that I would make a bundle more.

Man, was I wrong.

TRAINING CAMP ENDS

Camp ended with a big scrimmage in Port Angeles. I played pretty well. We had 13 guys, I was the injured-list guy who fakes an injury. And they let go Harold Fox, William Harris, and Larry Hollyfield.

When they let Hollyfield go, he really put on a show. He cried so hard, I told him he could have my position. He had arrived thinking he was a shoo-in because of the hype he received at UCLA—he was on a lot of big television games. He was a member of the Bruins teams with Bill Walton that went 60-0 and won national championships.

When he was cut, we thought he was going to kill himself. He cried like a little baby. I mean—vocally—he made loud sounds, like he was a victim.

I thought somebody had shot him.

CHAPTER 3

ROOKIE SEASON
(1973-74)

FINDING A HOME

When we got back from Port Angeles, Russell told me, "Boy, you can play, but all the positions are taken." He kept me around, so I needed a place to stay.

Everybody else lived up on Magnolia—all the big-timers. John Brisker lived in Bellevue, so Brisker took me over to see Bellevue. You could see deer running over on 148th and 156th. On Northeast Eighth, you would see all kinds of animals. Bellevue was like the country. Now I can't believe all the buildings over there. But I found a place: Pacifica Apartments. It's still standing. It had a view, and that was where everybody used to socialize and have parties. I moved into Bellevue as the season started.

CRAWL BEFORE YOU WALK

I clearly remember one of the first drills Russ put us through in those first days of the season. He said Red Auerbach did this once, and so he did it, too. He took the ball, threw it out, and we had to fight for it like it was a piece of gold. If you didn't get the ball, you had to do it until you got it. You could be there all day trying to get it.

I had on my knee pads. Everybody was running for the ball, and I crawled—I crawled for it and beat everyone there on my knees.

Russell cackled and said, "Look at the boy—that boy crawled for it. Boy, you can crawl faster than they can run." Crawling on my knees, I still got the ball on the first go, so I sat and watched as everyone else struggled on the floor.

The next day in the paper—when he was asked by a reporter about the drill—Russell was quoted as saying: "Oh, we don't use that [exercise] for any special reason . . . except that it's painful. We've been too easy on these guys. Nobody is throwing up."

Fred Brown hated this drill. Fred was a shooter. This was a drill for hungry guys who were trying to make the team. This wasn't a drill for a shooter. Russell would cackle and tell me, "Boy, that's what is going to keep you around."

He used to always make statements like that. He had a talent for complimenting you and putting you down in the same breath.

THE DANCING BEAR

Playing in Seattle for 13 years, Fred Brown was one of the best players ever to wear a Sonics uniform. But when I came in, Fred was still a bit round at the edges—he was a big boy. We used to call him "Fat Freddy, the Dancing Bear" because he was heavy at the time. Dancing Freddy.

I don't know why Freddy was heavy. But later he got down to about 175, and that's when he made the All-Star team. He lost the weight on the bike and by what I call push-aways—he'd push away from the table, and he got himself in good shape.

PAYING THE ROOKIE PRICE— AND KEEPING THE CHANGE

I was not making any money my rookie year, so I had a system for earning some extra paper. When we were on the road, when practice was over, I would go by everybody's door and take orders for sandwiches. I didn't mind it. I was a happy-go-lucky guy. I guess I was everybody's boy.

Anyway, we used to get about $45 or $50 a day in meal money, so this is what I would do. I used to take my meal money and put it in my pocket. Then, when I would take guys' orders for sandwiches, they would give me $10 or $20 for the sandwich and just say, "Keep the change." I liked that job—I was smart.

If I had a chance to go to 10 or 12 guys and they gave me $10 apiece, I would keep the change, get my own lunch paid for, have a little extra spending money, and take all my meal money home with me. When we'd go on a 14-day trip, I would come home with all my meal money.

WELCOME TO NEW YORK, NEW YORK

Every time we went to New York, we stayed at the Hyatt Regency hotel. They had a little ol' sandwich shop around the corner that sold Reuben sandwiches.

On one occasion, Jim McDaniels went with me to get the sandwiches, and he said, "Look here, man, you're from Rolling Fork, Mississippi. You don't know how to handle New York.

Man, I'm going to show you. You don't even know how to cross the street."

As he started to walk across the street, a taxi hit him and knocked the seven-footer about 20 feet in the air. I thought he was hurt, so I ran over and said, "Jim, Jim, Jim, you all right?"

He looked up and said, "You tell anybody, I'm going to kill you." He was trying to show me how to be cool. He said I was too country to walk the streets of New York, and then he got hit by a taxi cab.

He was real cool.

ATHOS, PORTHOS, AND ARAMIS

Jim McDaniels was part of the "Three Musketeers" along with John Brisker and Spencer Haywood.

Except, instead of the "Three Musketeers," I called them the "Three Millionaires." All three came from the ABA, and they had big contracts. They started that trend of players getting big money. When they came, the Sonics supposedly were getting three $1 million players.

Unlike the guys in the book, though, our Three Musketeers really didn't say that much to each other because they were all trying to rule. They were like the Dobermans down at the dog park trying to see who had the biggest teeth.

JAW BREAKERS

Russell used to make everybody mad at each other so we could have good practices. He enjoyed antagonizing everyone, and at his size, he was good at it. That led to the fight of my life. I had never seen two big guys over six foot five scrap in my life. After seeing it, I never wanted to see it again.

It was John Brisker and Joby Wright, a star player from Indiana University. Brisker was the top dog in practice, throwing his weight around. Joby was six foot nine, 250 or so—a very big, strong guy. One day in practice, they got into a serious confrontation.

Back in those days, the big superstar player controlled practice—we had three. In practice those three wanted it their way, which means, "Don't foul me." My big thing was to hack a guy's arm or hand in practice, but—when I used to see them—I used to go the other way.

So on this day, Brisker was throwing his weight around, and Joby wouldn't get back. Nobody could get involved because he was so strong. When Brisker hit him, he caught him with a right hand, and you could hear his jaw break—everything was dead still. You talk about afraid—everybody was afraid.

Joby grabbed his jaw and said, "Man, you broke my jaw." He also had four of his teeth loosened. We had to call the ambulance. It was about two or three weeks in practice before anybody bumped Brisker again. Joby ended up getting his jaw wired, and then he was cut later that year. I think that fight ruined Joby's career.

After the fight, Russell told the *Seattle Times*: "The next time the guys will realize that when they start a fight they'll have to finish it, so maybe they won't be so eager to start one."

I don't know why he said that—seems to me that Brisker finished it.

WHATEVER YOU WANT, MR. BRISKER

John Brisker could be so nice, but sometimes something snapped in him. I remember one day in practice, I blocked his shot from behind, and he turned around and slapped me—and he liked me. He immediately apologized, but I said, "No, no, no, I'm sorry."

I didn't want to get into a scrap with John—John was the man. I was just happy that he did not break my jaw—so I did not argue; I did not shout; I just apologized and moved on out of the way.

After practice, he took me to lunch, and again apologized for the way he reacted.

I reassured him (and my jaw): "John, no problem."

BARRIER BRISKER

If there was one thing I learned from those two incidents with Brisker, I knew that I was safe because he was on my team. The second most memorable fight of my life was when we were playing in Phoenix against the great Pat Riley. Just about everybody on the floor started fighting, and seven-foot-two Tom Burleson took off across the floor like Batman and dove on the entire crowd. That was a fun fight.

Riley wasn't as he is today, with slicked-back hair and cool clothes. Back then he had long hair and a mustache. He came off the bench trying to be tough, and Burleson just dove over his head, knocked him into the crowd. Now when I see Pat on the sideline, I just smile and think back to that fight. What a difference.

I was smart—I always got behind Brisker when a fight broke out. Ever since Brisker showed me he was the man by breaking Joby Wright's jaw, I got behind him. I knew no one was coming to mess with Brisker. I'd just hide behind him until the fight was over.

HURRICANE COWENS

The third best fight I ever saw was when we were playing the Boston Celtics. Tom Burleson got the ball in the post, and Dave

Cowens, who is only six foot eight, caught one of Tommy's elbows in the nose. Dave started howling and swinging and swinging. Oh man, what a fight.

Fred Brown and I were cool, we sat on the side, and we were yelling, "Get him. Get him."

We stayed out of the way, though. Everybody over six foot eight was involved, but we little guys stayed back.

Those big guys, boy—Dave Cowens didn't want to stop. They just kept going and going. Dave Cowens was like a big John Brisker. Once you got him started, he wouldn't stop coming at you. I would say Dave got the best of it, but Tom got him good in the nose.

SLICK, SLICK, WE WANT SLICK

At the beginning of my rookie year, I was not as much coming off the bench as I was doing all the chores. I was more like a gofer. I did everything for everybody, because I was just happy to be there.

We started losing early in the season. We were 6-14 after 20 games, even though Russell virtually guaranteed that we were going to make the playoffs because of our talent.

Anyway, when we started out so poorly, the fans would say, "Remember the little bald-headed kid in training camp? Why don't you play him?"

Whenever we would come back home, the fans would start chanting: "Slick, Slick, we want Slick."

And Russell would get up and chant with the fans, "Slick, Slick, we want Slick."

Then he would look at me and say, "The fans want you to get in there, better get in there."

I'd jump up, and he'd say, "Sit down, boy."

I thought it was funny. It became a little game. He would hear the fans, and he'd start chanting with them—soon I laughed, because I knew he wasn't going to put me in.

BILL BRIDGES FALLING DOWN

Spencer Haywood could dunk—and in this game, he slammed the best I ever saw him put down. It was on Bill Bridges—Bill was one of those strong, old-time, good ol' boys who didn't back off anybody. He played for the Los Angeles Lakers.

Well, on this night, Spencer picked up the ball with that one hand. He had what I call "double-jointed fingers." That's not the right term, but that's what I called it. You look at your finger, and everybody has one, two, three sections to their fingers. But Spencer had four. He had that extra knuckle, which I called "double-jointed," but I should call *double-knuckled*. He had big ol' hands.

Anyway, Spencer picked up that ball at the free throw line, and Bill Bridges was at his back. Bill was big, like six foot eight, 240—he was an enforcer. Bill Bridges started the enforcer role before Maurice Lucas. Spencer picked him up on his back and just gunned him down with a dunk. The rim just rattled. The entire arena was stunned.

Bill got up and started fighting, and they were swinging. Boy, they were going at it. Bill hit Spencer and knocked him flat on the ground. Then he hit Mahdi Abdul-Rahman and knocked him out cold. Then Emmette Bryant tried to step in, and Bridges flipped him off the court.

As usual, I found somebody to hide behind—but I would have to say that that was the most spectacular dunk I've ever seen by anybody.

FIRST BIG GAME

The game that first got me noticed was on December 1, 1973.

Russ said to me, "Boy, you been walking around practice, talking all this trash and telling me you can play. I am going to see if you can play tonight."

Once again, I thought he was messing with me and I wasn't going to play. This particular night, though, he said, "I am going to see tonight."

I got nervous. We were in Atlanta to play against "Pistol" Pete Maravich. It was the Pistol Pete show at that time. I had played sporadically—at the end of blowouts up to this point—but this was my first game playing big minutes. We weren't winning, so Russ was trying to find some combination that worked. He had labeled that time of year "crisis time," because if we did not pick it up soon we were going to miss the playoffs. We had lost to Milwaukee by 34 points the previous game.

So Russ played me against the Atlanta Hawks—a game on national television—against Pistol Pete.

To a guy who played at Xavier University in New Orleans (Pete played at Louisiana State), Pete was like the Bill Russell of guards and the god of ball-handling. Little kids—black or white—all wanted to be Pistol Pete. We saw him as a great basketball player, but more like a white Globetrotter. He could do anything with the ball.

I was proud to go against him in that first game and try to make some things happen against him. To me, it was a privilege just to play against these guys. Pete would come down the court, and—what I liked about him when he came down on the fast break—he'd lock the ball behind his back and hide it so you couldn't see it.

My coaches in college always taught me that when you are defending the fast break, fake one way, and then go back and get

Slick wearing his favorite attire.
From the Donald Watts Collection

the pass. But when I faked against Pete, I didn't see the ball any more, and he finger rolled it—the whole bench laughed at me.

Like Russell said afterward, though: "Slick, he's done that to a lot of people, don't feel bad."

Even though Pete made me look silly a couple of times, I was able to pick his pocket a few times because I was quicker.

Bob Hopkins—my college coach and later an assistant with the Sonics—remembers that game:

"I hadn't seen Slick since he talked to Bill Russell in my office that day. And the next time I saw Slick he was going against Pistol Pete there in Atlanta. He came in and took the ball from him three straight times. And two times he stole it. I mean, Slick did something that you rarely ever see. He did something we called the reverse move, where you fake one way, then turn the other way, and when you turn, he's got the ball. Pete didn't know what hit him. The next time, Slick slapped at the ball and missed and went around him, and Pete tried to go past him, and Slick knocked it away from behind. I mean, he put on a dazzling show. And Coach said to me after the game, 'The boy ain't bad. I'm gonna have to rein him in and tone him down a little bit, because he talks the game too, but the boy ain't bad.' Russ told me confidentially, 'The guy really has a lot of confidence, Hop. The guy can really make things happen.'"

I also scored 21 points in that game in just 17 minutes. I scored 11 in the fourth quarter, and afterward Russell just looked at me and said, "Boy, you don't know what the hell you are doing out there."

Later he also told me: "You're doing things I haven't seen since K.C. Jones."

I idolized K.C. Jones; it was one of the proudest moments of my career.

WHY PEOPLE HATE LAWYERS

My lawyer was from Chicago. I signed an agreement for him to get me drafted—then he dropped me because I wasn't drafted. When Hopkins called Russell and got me a job, my lawyer didn't even know I had a job.

After seeing me drop 21 points on Atlanta, he sent me a bill. First he called me and said, "Congratulations." Then he called Zollie Volchok and Bob Walsh and told them I owed him 10 percent of my check. I had to pay him, too. I couldn't believe it.

A CAPITAL DEFENSE

After Atlanta, we went to D.C. to play against Dave Bing, Archie Clark, Wes Unseld, and Elvin Hayes. Three of those guys are Hall of Famers now. It was the grand opening of the Capital Centre, the Bullets' new arena.

It was the first state-of-the-art arena. I remember getting on the Washington beltway and getting lost on the way to the arena. Sometimes we would rent cars. I remember getting on that freeway and going around that circle—I thought we were going to end up in Baltimore or Virginia somewhere. I still don't know where I was when I got there, because it was on the outskirts of the city. Everyone was wondering why the place was built so far away from everything. It didn't help that the grand opening invited traffic jams. We barely made it to the game.

Anyway, Russell put me in against the Bullets. Archie Clark shook me up in the bleachers on one crossover, but I took about three or four from him.

We even talk about it now. I have so much respect for Archie because I thought Archie was one of the most underrated stars in the NBA. I thought he was much like Hal Greer—one of those players who didn't get much attention—I thought Archie was a great player. He invented the crossover. We called it "shake and bake." I bet Tim Hardaway got his crossover from studying Archie Clark.

In the game, Elvin Hayes went up for a shot, but I snuck in and stole the ball from behind his head, then went in for the layup. I had 24 points in that game, plus 11 rebounds and six assists.

I almost had the game winner, too. With a few seconds left, I stole the ball from Archie. Spencer picked it up and threw it to me, but as I was going in for a lay-up, Elvin Hayes blocked my shot from behind. John Brisker got the loose ball and shot it, but Elvin blocked that shot, too. The Big E could really play. We lost by two.

More people watched that game than any other basketball game in Maryland history. They had 17,000 that night. That was big-time then. No other place we went to had 17,000.

BEING BIG TIME

After that Bullets game, Abe Pollin—the owner of the Washington Bullets—came up and told me, "Young man, you can play. I wish we had some players like you."

I'll never forget that night because they had a party after the game for the opening of the Capital Centre, and Abe Pollin invited me to the executive suite after the game. I went up there to eat and socialize—it was my first feeling of being Big Time.

Later, Russ asked me on the plane, "Boy, you know what the f--- were you doing out there tonight?"

I said, "I told you, Coach—if you can coach, I can play."

"Get the f--- out of here," he said.

FIRST START

When we came back home, after losing five of six games on that trip, Big Bill promised that he was going to make some changes. He was threatening to trade some people, but at the time, the only change he could make was in the starting lineup.

So he inserted me in there, next to Fred. In my first start, I had 12 points and nine assists, but we lost to Detroit by two.

Afterwards, Pistons coach Ray Scott told the *Seattle Post-Intelligencer*, "Seattle played like hell. They really worked out there. I'll tell you who I was impressed with tonight for the Sonics—Slick Watts."

After starting a few games, Russell said, "Slick is very valuable to us. He makes things happen out there. He's the only player here who can change the tempo of the game."

FIRST WIN AS A STARTER

I was now in the starting lineup. We went down to Los Angeles. We hadn't beaten the Lakers in 13 straight games, and we hadn't beaten them at The Forum in 20 straight—since 1971. On this night, behind my hustle, we beat them 115-111. I had 14 points, 10 assists, five rebounds—and even though I was wearing a Sonics uniform, I was a crowd favorite. I think it was my bald head more than my play, though.

Afterwards, Russ said: "One thing I do know—hustle is a talent."

"That was oh so sweet," I told Don Fair of the *Post-Intelligencer* after the game. "Maybe everything is falling into place now."

I meant for the team—but it was for me as well.

CONTROVERSY

Right around this time, a story came out in *Sports Illustrated* that the year before the Sonics had intentionally dumped a game against the Philadelphia 76ers to get Tom Nissalke fired as coach. The Sixers won just nine games the entire season.

In the story, the author, Bob Briner, the former general manager of the Dallas Chaparrals, wrote:

"Even flat-out fixing of games has become nothing but another fact of salary negotiation—or renegotiations, as it is known these days. Tom Nissalke broke his contract with the Dallas Chaparrals after we had given him his first crack at being a head coach, to take the post at Seattle last year. When a few SuperSonics found Nissalke too tough for their high-salaried style, they boasted—even to referees—that they would lose enough to get him fired. It took, finally, a dumped game against the woebegone Philadelphia 76ers to get rid of Nissalke."

There were many rumors going around. Tom had a reputation as a real demanding coach. Brisker and all these guys were the new cowboys in town. People said they didn't play to win.

We didn't really talk about it in the locker room. At that time, maybe some of the big hitters did. Remember, I still didn't matter at that time, so I didn't get too much into it. Still, I don't think anybody dumped it.

They just tune you out and go out freelancing and play—let the chemistry go. I don't think they actually went out and let someone score on them.

They just lost all team chemistry, organization, and ability to play together. They just played a little different. However, that would have been a good game for them to get somebody fired. It's funny how we used to approach playing Cleveland. We used to say if Cleveland beat us, Coach is going to be fired. So we used to play hard against Cleveland.

ICED

After 25 straight starts I was playing really well, but when we went to Phoenix, Russell did not even play me. The Big Fella iced me. He tightened up the headband.

He was playing with my head, saying: "Boy, you may think you did something, but you didn't. Even though you think you did, you haven't done sh--."

And he kept benching me, even though we were losing.

Then the fans started to chant my name, and Russell would look at me and say, "Slick, the fans want you, you better get in there."

I'd play like someone had cut off my head. What I did well was disrupt the opponent's offensive rhythm. Russell used me as a tempo setter. Slowly but surely, the legend started to grow.

At one point, Russell told the newspapers, "If Slick continues, he is a real top contender for NBA rookie of the year. He does as much as Ernie DiGregorio and is better defensively. Slick's job is to run our offense, and that he does."

In my rookie year I was second-team All-Rookie team. But Ernie D, he won the rookie of the year. I think I would have won it if the Big Fella didn't put me on ice for 25 games.

POINT GUARDING

Spencer used to come to me and say: "Slick, you know who your goddam meal ticket is? Bring the ball over to this side." Spencer wouldn't hesitate to tell you, "Bring it over here."

I would take it over there, too. If you wanted to be successful as a point guard, you had to cater to your stars.

I played with Truck Robinson in New Orleans, who was a good rebounder. I used to enjoy talking trash to him and playing him one on one after practice. Old Mike Bantom, too—he used to do the same thing. He used to have that little man-big man ego going on. He used to say, "You are a mouse in the house. I'll post you up."

That was fun going after the big boys in practice. The offense came through me, so the big boys all liked me, because when I got them the ball, they got more shots—and bigger contracts. If you were a guard who passed, you had many friends. That was why I felt like a player and a fan, because I was a friendly passer. Mike Newlin sees me now and hugs me—all because I got him a ton of open shots.

CHAPTER 4

BILL RUSSELL

I think it is safe to say that Bill Russell and I had a love-hate relationship. Most players had a hate-hate relationship with Russ, but I had a certain affinity for him—mostly because when I got to Seattle I thought he was like a god.

Although he would probably never admit it, I think Russ has a special place in his heart for me—if Russ has a heart. It may be a very small place, but I think it is there. Mostly, I think it's there because Russ discovered me.

He was brought in for two reasons: He was supposed to get a handle on these big egos—specifically Spencer, John Brisker, and Jim McDaniels. As I said before, this was the beginning of the big contracts—the million-dollar contracts—and guys had million-dollar egos. If anybody could control those egos, it was a man who had won 11 championships in 13 seasons. In fact, when Russell first got to town, the media had named him "The Dictator."

I think Sam had good intentions when he brought Russell in. Sam wanted a winner. He was a community guy. Russell was supposed to be a father figure and have a stronger command over those guys. I don't think Sam really wanted to get rid of them at first, I think he wanted to keep them all. With Russell being "The Man," he figured winning breeds winning. It didn't really matter the way these kids changed because of the money. He wanted Russell to put his finger on those big three and make it work.

Even Russell, in his first training camp, told the *Seattle Times*, "We've got a lot of talent on this team. We're going to surprise a lot of people. If I didn't mean it, I wouldn't say it. Look, I'm not a great coach. But there are certain things I can get this team to do that will make it a winner."

But then Sam found out that even with Russell—or maybe because of Russell, though that wouldn't be discovered until much later—the money wasn't getting it done. He signed these three guys, and he thought it meant victory. Then he found out it wasn't working. It didn't happen. Then, since Russell couldn't make these three win, Sam wanted Russell to trim the payroll and get rid of them.

That was the second reason Russell was brought in—he had enough power to get rid of these guys without the fans booing, because if Bill Russell doesn't like them, then maybe they were not winners. So he got rid of them. Russell was supposed to determine who would go and who would stay. As it turned out, they all went, but that was more about personality conflicts than money. Actually, before it was all over, everybody had a personality conflict with the Big Fella. Russ is something else. He is a piece of work. Yet when he first arrived, everybody was completely in awe of him.

Russell had it in his head that he wanted the Boston concept, where he had many equal parts playing cohesive basketball, as opposed to a few stars mixed with role players. He wanted to be Boston *West*. What Russ never figured out was that there is only one Boston—and it is located in the East.

By the end, Russell had alienated virtually every one of his players. Worse, he had alienated the entire city. During home

Big Fella running the show.
From the Donald Watts Collection

games at the Seattle Coliseum, he was booed regularly. Things are different now. He goes to home games at KeyArena and gets cheered again. Enough time has passed. People have forgiven and forgotten.

Or perhaps just forgotten. Again, he is a Hall of Fame icon. Back then, though, when he was coaching, he was nobody's favorite.

In a way, I think the city felt betrayed. When he became the coach, everybody expected the Great Bill Russell to lead the Sonics to a championship. After all, he had won his entire career with Boston, why wouldn't he keep winning? It was only a matter of time. The city fell in love with his reputation. If Bill Russell says a player can't play, then a player can't play. If Bill Russell says something must be a certain way, then it must be a certain way. Yet it became increasingly clear that after Russ had ended the careers of talented players like John Brisker and Jim McDaniels, and had shipped away skilled players like Leonard Gray because they could not get along, that Bill Russell was more about Bill Russell than he was about winning. It took the city a few years to figure Big Bill out, but once it did, Seattle agreed with few of his methods.

To this day, I hear that when Russ has a speaking engagement, he talks about me for 15 minutes. So I don't really feel badly telling some stories about him.

WALKING TALL

When I first got to town, the television stations were everywhere, thrilled because the Great Bill Russell had come to town, carrying his baseball bat over his shoulder, a big man with a stick, like *Walking Tall*.

He was cackling on TV all over the place. The bat was a front thing. He was letting people know that he was coming for business—that he was coming to turn things around. It was an image. That was the way he portrayed it—Bill Russell with a baseball bat.

SEATTLE CELTICS

Red Auerbach, who coached Russ in Boston, had a philosophy that we all had a position. The shooters shoot, the passers pass, the rebounders rebound—everybody had a role. Russell coached that way, too.

Some nights, he would get on me about shooting. "That is not your role, boy, you are K.C. Jones."

Fred Brown was supposed to be Sam Jones. Leonard Gray and Hal Fox were supposed to stand by the goal and get offensive rebounds like Tom Heinsohn and Bailey Howell. Tal Skinner was supposed to play like Satch Sanders used to play. Each of us was to represent a piece of Boston's pie (of course, he never got to the point where he said which player was supposed to be Bill Russell. He wanted Tommy Burleson and the guys to be shot blockers, but he didn't think anybody could do the things he did as a player).

In fact, we used to run the same plays the Celtics did. We used to run the same play where John Havlicek came off a double pick, and the center would hand him the ball for a shot from the top of the key—except Russell substituted Fred Brown for Havlicek.

I remember when I was growing up watching those plays in the '60s. Then I came up here in the '70s, I had to learn those same plays that I saw in high school on TV. Unfortunately, they didn't work—we didn't win 13 championships. But he was the first coach to get the Sonics to the playoffs, and that was his concept—*do what Boston did.*

HALLOWED GROUND

The Big Fella used to tell us he loved the city of Boston, but I always thought he had issues with Boston. He would tell us stories of going to the restaurants and not being served because he was black. And he told us how the white players on the Celtics team stood behind him and would go to the restaurants that would serve all of them. They would eat as a team. He used to talk about the team concept a lot, because race relations was an experience he had in the '60s, being one of only two black players on the team. Personally, I think he was affected by it. It made him stronger, and then I thought, mentally, it made him tougher.

He is kind of protective, but his situation in Boston was similar to Jackie Robinson's in Brooklyn. I always tell him that I don't feel sorry for him, because we all went through that. You have to let it go. Growing up in the '50s and '60s in the deep South, we all went through periods of racism. But you have to let that go.

And I don't think he can let it go.

What's funny is, when we played Boston, I thought Russell became the best coach in the world. For some reason, he prepared us well to play Boston. He said the game didn't mean anything to him, but for some reason we always played well. And he would come into the locker room pleased whenever we beat Boston. Russell used to find ways to call you things even when he was praising you.

His favorite phrase was: "You bunch of gutless wonders." Sometimes he would change "gutless wonders" to "gutless MFs."

Whenever we beat Boston, though, we were just "gutless wonders."

MIND GAMES

Team concepts and plays weren't the only thing that Russell brought from Boston. He also used to steal Red Auerbach's motivational tactics. One thing Red used to do when he wanted to motivate players was tell them they weren't going to play. When you got in Red's doghouse, Red would turn around and wouldn't speak to you for a week. Then all of a sudden you would be the first man in the starting lineup. And it would really catch you off guard.

Somtimes players would shoot the lights out when he did that, and Red would say, "See, that works." Russell used to use many of those same tricks on us.

One day, Talvin Skinner didn't practice very well. Russ told Tal he wasn't rebounding. He called him gutless. Oh, Russ really got on him. Tal had his head down, and he really thought he would be cut. The next night, he told Tal, "You'll never play for me again." Tal had water in his eyes.

Then that night, the public address announcer came on and said, "Starting at small forward, Talvin Skinner." Tal turned around and looked at me.

Russell said, "That's your name, boy, get out there." Tal must have had 18 points and 12 rebounds that night. Russ could motivate by making you think you were in the doghouse, although you weren't in the doghouse.

He'd pull that, and then he'd wink and say, "I got him, didn't I?"

HOME SOUR HOME

The funny thing about Russell feeling good about returning to Boston and beating the Celtics is that he used to hate when one of his players returned home.

This was something Russ was good at: If you went to your home to play a game, and all your fans and family and friends were at the game, and you had the most tickets, you might not play at all. Whew, he was good at that. I don't know why he did that. He just loved to do it. If you had all your family come 500 miles, you'd just sit.

So one night we were in Kansas City, where Leonard Gray was from, and he didn't play Leonard. Man, I thought we were going to have to move the dressing room. Leonard was seething. Oh man, he was mad. Water was running down his cheeks he was so mad. When a big man has water in his eyes, you know he is mad. Boy was he pissed—and Russell knew he was pissed.

Big Fella just looked at him and popped his knuckles.

MY MAMA HAS TO SEE ME ON TV

When we played in New Orleans, I told my mama, who was living in Mississippi, "Don't come see me play. Don't y'all come, because I don't know what is going to happen."

I wasn't going to let anybody come up when Russell was coaching. My philosophy was keep your family away from the game with Big Bill around, because Big Bill thought you were showing him up and he would bench you. If he didn't bench you because you were a star, mistakes were very much in the front of his mind. He didn't have the patience for you if you were playing in front of your home people. Your head must balloon when your family is here, he thought. More to the point—if I missed a shot in New York, it was a part of the game; if I missed a shot in New Orleans, I was showing off.

Your first shot—make it or not—he'd tell you, "That is not what I want."

He was just messing with you. I could never figure it out.

PLAIN ADVICE

Back then, the players weren't allowed to sit up in first class on flights.

All the players used to sit in coach; the head coach and the general manager would sit up front. I always thought it was funny that the coach never sat in coach. Back in those days they let you know who was in charge.

When Russ felt like talking, though, he'd call me up front to sit next to him, and he'd tell me things. He didn't talk to many people. Perhaps he thought I had promise—that he could mold me. He was real deep and fancied himself a philosopher. You'd be sitting back in coach, and he'd say, "Come here, boy. Sit down."

He had a lot on his mind; he wanted to talk. He was a guy who didn't want to share with you unless he felt like it. He was never a guy who would hold a conversation if you wanted to talk to him. He would have to call you to him. He would never let you get comfortable. He always wanted to be one up.

Whenever I asked him for more money, Russ's favorite thing to say to me was, "Boy, whatever you were before you got your money, that is what you will be when you get your money. If you were a butthole when you were poor, you are just going to be a rich butthole."

Then he'd cackle and add, "Money ain't going to help you; money ain't going to change you."

Then I'd say, "Coach, why is everybody else getting paid then?"

SPEAKING OF WHICH . . .

Coach Russell would never invite you to his house for a party, but he was never afraid to show you all the things that he had accomplished: his nice place, his big whirlpool, everything. He would walk through his office and show you everything—and he knew I was like a kid in a candy shop. He was the man.

He would say, "Now look at that, you keep playing, boy, you will have something like this one day," then cackle some more.

BE GONE WITH YOU

Perhaps one of the things that made Coach such a good defensive player was that he was always trying to read people.

He always told me, "Jerry West would turn the corner. Most centers would run after him. You see, Jerry turns the corner, and instead of running this way, after him, I would run over this way and meet him. I knew angles." Then, he would look at you— waiting.

And I'd say, "Yeah, Coach, that was smart."

He always wanted to say something deep to you. I have to admit, though, that was kind of smart. However, after Russ made his points, he would get tired of you.

"Get the hell out of here," he'd say. "Get out of here, I'm tired of you." Then he would wave his hand and tell you to get up, and I'd mosey back to sit with everyone else.

PLAYING IT SAFE

One day on the plane, some guys said John Brisker was back in coach and tried to hit on one of Russell's girls. Afterwards, he went deeper—*much deeper*—on the bench. He was already the eighth man. Then he dropped to the fifteenth man, and soon he didn't even dress out. Big Fella didn't like you talking to his friends on the plane.

They always sat back there in coach, smiling, and I would just say, "Hi, who are you with?"

"I'm Coach's friend."

And I'd say, "Oh, I'm sorry. I didn't know. I didn't even speak to you. I'm so sorry. Tell Coach I said hi."

NEW YORK STATE OF MIND

One of the deals Russ had with Sam Schulman when he became coach was that Russ would have total control over the organization, and nobody—not even Sam—could question him.

Russ made all the decisions on where we'd stay. Wherever the Big Fella liked, that was where we stayed in those days. And Russ loved New York. Matter of fact, when we played Boston, we would get out of Boston and go to New York, and then go to Boston the day of the game. He loved New York.

CONTROLLING THE MEDIA

Being the big guy that he was, Russ had a way of instilling fear and controlling the media. Because he knew we read the papers, he would send messages through the media as well.

Sometimes, when he would bench me just because he felt like benching me, he would tell the media that I broke a team rule. He was letting the media know he was in control. He would say I didn't play the game I should have played.

Then the next game he would praise you, make you feel like you were All-World. One game he said I had one of the best games he'd ever coached, one of the best games he had ever seen a guy under six foot two play. He made that statement after playing with the great Bob Cousy.

He would put you down, but he had a way of lifting you up. I think he thought he was a father figure—it gave him an excuse to treat you like a son.

TRICKS TO DEALING WITH RUSSELL

In his own way, Russell intimidated me, but at the same time, he didn't. It was kind of like Kareem, how I was intimidated by him until I learned he was human—same thing with Russell.

My first year, I was so impressed, eyes so big with so much excitement, just meeting him was intimidating. But then I started listening to him and starting sitting with him and talking with him. I found out how he started to do things—how he used that old Boston mentality on you sometimes, playing mind games.

I found out this guy has issues, and I didn't really like that. I think Fred Brown noticed that much earlier. He didn't play Russell's game. He was a different guy. I don't think Russ ever did intimidate Fred. Leonard Gray was a hard nut to crack, too.

I soon discovered that when he stared at you, you should stare back. Stare at him right back. And then he would bust up laughing and say, "This sh-- could go on forever." After that, he was cool.

He would give you that look, and he would be like my Doberman; if you are submissive to him, then he had you, he had you the rest of the week. If you stared back at him, hung in there for 10 minutes and just stared him down, he would start laughing. He had issues. He always wanted to break you. Afterwards, though, he would respect you more and reveal all his tales.

RUSSELL VS. SPENCER HAYWOOD

Russ almost immediately didn't get along with John Brisker and Jim McDaniels. But from the very start he took to Spencer. I think he saw that maybe it was Spencer's city, too, and maybe he could make him his son. Spencer told me that Russell treated him like a son at first. "We hung out, we was tight," Spencer told me.

Russell had a way of making you his favorite, but you had to fall under his guidelines. When I became his favorite, I was pretty good at it, because I was from Mississippi. When you are from Mississippi, you learn to adjust because of the way you have been brought up around people who are supposed to be above you. So I called Coach "Sir" and stuff like that. One had that mentality if you were raised in the South.

Spencer was a Mississippi-born guy too, but Spencer spent some time in Detroit, and he had that city toughness in him. I think their true personalities began to clash. They were like two captains of the same ship. I think when you showed Russ that you had any issues that were bigger than his issues, then it was like water and oil—they just wouldn't mix. You could see it at practice; things began to change. Spencer began to complain, and Russ started to sit him. As a team, we didn't think that would ever happen, that Russell would ever get him out of town. But he pulled it off—Big Fella got him out of town.

DISSECTING RUSSELL

Russell's thing is to be like Michael Jordan. His image is, "I'm too big."

Like, if Fred Brown signs an autograph, then Russell wouldn't. It was one of those reverse psychology things. At first he wouldn't even accept his nomination into the Hall of Fame. That is another statement altogether; but it is a sly statement.

Everything he does, he does for a reason. The people and the media think that he has shied away from the publicity, but that is his way of getting you to talk about him. I understand him now. He couldn't stand me, but he liked me.

In some articles he would say, "Slick is one of the greatest players I ever coached."

You ask him now, and he'll say, "I never said that."

But I know he did—I saved the articles.

CHANGING DYNAMICS

My relationship with Russell began to change when I felt like I was being underpaid for my contributions to the team. However, Russell—ever one to hold something over you—didn't want to pay me.

On one east coast road trip, I was on fire. I thought I was ready to blossom. When we came home, I asked for some money . . . that's when the issues started to arise. That's when Big Fella said: "Slick, your headband is getting too tight, huh?"

RUSSELL'S PROMISE

Russell made me a promise one day. He might deny it, but he made me a promise.

He told me, "Sam is not treating you right now, but as long as I am here, I am going to get you a million dollars."

He made me that promise in 1975-76, when I was rolling.

That was just before he left. I believed him because I was star-struck. I thought he was indestructible. I thought he was going to be here nine years, and he would get me my money. He said, "Just be patient, boy, I am going to take care of you." Then Sam called him in and surprised him—he was gone.

I was upset because I backed off when I could have gotten some money. Archie Clark tells me to this day I would have had a great 15- or 16-year career if Russell hadn't got hold of me. Archie knew how Russell tried to control me. He used to give me my props.

But I told Archie, "No, he didn't get in my head, he just controlled the pocket book."

But when I got a chance to get paid, it was too late—Russ was gone.

NO HARD FEELINGS

I see Russell sometimes. Actually, I often see Russell, and he always says the same thing: "Boy, what you doing? Come here, boy."

And I'll say, "Hey, Coach."

He'll always be my coach.

But you can forget about him apologizing for anything that happened in the past. Big Bill thinks so much he probably doesn't remember saying anything he ever said to me.

LOOKING BACK

I don't know how we made the playoffs because we certainly had some issues.

Big Fella was more than a coach, that's for sure. He was just so tied up in trying to get everybody to be like him or be like

Boston. This is what I hate about that system. Not everyone can be Bill Gates with computers. Just because Bill Gates has 60 billion dollars, it doesn't mean that we should reach for that amount. Russell has a ton of championships; but that doesn't make him the authority on winning or losing.

I still think how you play the game is important. Yes, winning is good, but what I tell the kids is it's how you play the game that makes the player. If you play with your heart and you sweat—you are a winner. Many people who have championships will never be winners. I know that personally.

There are people in this town who have rings, but they are not champs. I won't name them because that would be disrespectful, but in life, they are not champs. They are mean, hateful. If you drop $10 in your own house, they're the types who pick it up and steal it.

That ain't no champ.

RUSSELL'S DOWNFALL

Russell was pushed out I think probably because he lost some of the guys because of how he approached things. People get tired of being annihilated or intimidated. In a marriage, if you denigrate your wife all the time, one day you will find a letter saying, "I just can't take it no more."

It got to a point where many people couldn't deal with him. Many people would challenge him to the point where they wanted to fight him. There is something called God that I fear, but I fear no man. I am a God-fearing man, but that is it. I know we can't change things, and God knows Bill Russell can't, either.

CHAPTER 5

1974-75

The year 1974-75 was huge for me and for the Sonics. That year, Russell lost his emotions, then gave me a big ol' hug—it was only the second time the franchise had enjoyed a winning record—sending us, for the first time, into the playoffs.

No one expected us to make it past the first round, but we raced into the Western Conference Finals, taking Rick Barry's Golden State Warriors to a sixth game. That extraordinary season yielded one of the only occasions that Russ let his guard down and gave me that big ol' hug.

SOMETIMES, LIFE IS FAIR

I would not really say that I was super big-time in Seattle yet, but I was certainly on my way up the ladder. Much of that was due to Don Fair, a reporter for the *Seattle Post-Intelligencer*. I call Don Fair "The Slick Watts Maker." Because he knew that I respected people, he gave me the benefit of the doubt. I could do

Getting "the hug" from the Big Fella.
From the Donald Watts Collection

no wrong. "Slick made a beautiful pass, but Leonard dropped it," Don would write. I could have hit Leonard in the back of the head, and Don would have written that Leonard should have moved his head out of the way of my pass.

I knew how to respect a person's livelihood. I knew it was Don's job to write and my job to play. Back then, the reporters rode the team bus and flew with us because we were all flying commercial. If he was on that bus, I didn't sit in the corner and try to act cool. The more he wrote—the more people would come see us. I understood that, and I understood that Don had a job to do. Fred Brown was suspicious of the media; he never could get along with the reporters and never really liked them. I got along with reporters just as I got along with everybody else.

Michael Jackson says, "Why can't people just leave me alone?" I never understood that. You are the one on that stage doing all that singing, all that arching your back and shaking your hips, so you have to expect people to want to talk to you. I didn't mind people talking to me. I think Don Fair saw that, and that's why he treated me so well.

THE VOICE

Bob Blackburn—the voice of the Sonics—who has a banner hanging from the ceiling in Key Arena, was another "Slicks Watts Maker." Bob used to embellish things so well on the radio that he made me seem like a giant.

I once boarded the plane, and the stewardess saw me and asked, "Do you know that guy named Slick Watts?"

"I think so."

"Where is he? I want to meet him, I want to meet him."

So I told her, "I'm Slick Watts."

"No, he is about six foot ten. I listen to Bob Blackburn on the radio, and he must be big because Bob Blackburn says so."

When Bob would say, "Slick Watts got the rebound," she thought I was a tall, dominating guy because of the way he described the play. She didn't think I was me. All the guys on the plane told her that I was who I said I was, but she still didn't believe it.

"Bob Blackburn talks about you like you are a seven-footer."

Bob Blackburn made me a seven-footer, and I can never thank him enough for that.

I had to get out my license and show her my name before she believed me.

ROTATING PRACTICES

Sand Point Naval Air Station was our designated place for practices, but Russell and Bob Walsh were determined (along with Sam Schulman and Zollie Volchok) to keep the community involved. Because remember: We were the only pro team in town back then.

Therefore, we would go to different high schools and practice, which was a treat for the schools. They would have an assembly, and we would practice and scrimmage.

That would be good for the community, and we could play in front of crowds, which made the guys work harder at practice because nobody wanted to be shown up in front of a bunch of people.

ASSIST

During the regular season, I was seventh in the league in assists, averaging 6.1 per game. Archie Clark was right behind me at 5.6 per game. I also was fourth in the league in steals with 2.32 per game.

I've always thought that the NBA is backwards—they list the leading scorer first in a box score or on television. Scoring is the easy part of the game. Shooters just sit around and shoot shots. That's not work to be the high scorer.

I can go with rebounds because that is real work, but they should have defensive stops or something as a statistic. That is real work. I would look at Fred Brown sometimes, and he wouldn't even break a sweat—no sweat anywhere. He was not beaten up—no bruises. He wasn't crippled—no going in the training room and icing down.

I used to go to the trainer and have ice everywhere because I used to attack the middle. They would close on me and bang me in every direction. Right, left, boom, boom—when two big men close in that middle, even if you pass it out, you still get hit, and the referee would never catch them. Bone-shaking hits. Elbows might cut you. The other guy might catch you with his knee. In the heat of action, you didn't feel it. When you got home, though, you put ice here and ice there. I see why guys don't penetrate anymore—it is tough in that middle.

Then I'd pick up the paper the next morning, and Fred would get all the glory because he took and made some jump shots.

BREAKING DOWN THE LEGEND

My first year in the league, I was terrified of Kareem Abdul-Jabbar. When I saw him, my move was to turn around and go back from whence I came. He was more intimidating to me than Bill Russell being my coach, because Kareem was bigger than life.

I went to a small school, watching Lew Alcindor on TV when he played for UCLA. Being able to get to the pros and play against him, I thought he was the biggest alien I had ever seen. I had a good scoop shot, but when I saw Kareem, I said, "No, Sir," and I would turn around immediately.

So my second year in the league, I went in for a shot against Kareem, went right up against his body, and he ducked his head. And I thought, "Oh, wow!"

I found out that Kareem could not block a shot unless he took a step or he came to help from the weak side. As great as he was, he had a weakness. He loved to block shots from the weak side—he loved to help—but if you went right at him, he didn't block shots very well. All those years I had been scared of this guy, and he had a weakness.

It is funny when you find out these guys are human. This is a good lesson for a young fan learning basketball—hey, all players are actually human.

BLACK FEET

Russell controlled everything. He even chose our tennis shoes. We had those black tennis shoes like they had in Boston. I hated them. I thought they were the ugliest shoes in the world, but he had us wearing them. Some of us came in with little shoe contracts, so we'd have to wear that company's shoes. Yet, if they were white, Russell would look at you and say, "You better paint them black."

ROOMMATES

Traveling back then wasn't like today where players get their own luxury rooms. Back in the day, we used to share rooms. Russ was such a control freak that he chose our roommates. He would actually use another Boston concept.

Russell's Boston concept was that I was the point guard, and Tommy Burleson was the center. Russell felt that he and Bob Cousy made that Celtics team click. So he put Tommy and I together on the road, hoping that instead of watching TV we would talk hoops and become like Bob Cousy and the Big Fella.

We would talk hoops, but Russ hoped that we would develop the camaraderie where the game was run from the center of the court with your point guard and center. He would put the shooting guard and the power forward together so they could think about setting picks. Russell hoped that the forward would want to set picks for the guard because they shared a room and got to be friends. He put you in the room together so you developed respect for each other.

It was almost like a marriage—without the lovemaking.

SWITCHEROO TABOO

We never would have considered switching roommates after he had assigned our rooms. You didn't play that game. Russ was the man, and you didn't mess with Coach's decisions. He let us know what city we were playing in, what city we were staying in, he had Frank Furtado make all the room reservations—and that was his word.

Sometimes Big Guy would switch us up. He would put Tommy and me together on one trip, then Fred and me the next. He always had the starters together, so you would get to like each other.

Russ had an anecdote from when he was playing—after practice they would all go to the movies.

"You know what, Slick?" he would say. "We didn't even tell each other what movie we were going to. But I used to look up, and we all would be sitting there in the same movie . . . ack, ack, ack." He thought that was amazing—the whole team would be sitting there in the theater because they thought alike.

That's why he had us rooming together that way: so we would think alike.

FAVORITE ROOMMATE

I liked rooming with Dean Tolson because I could always kick him out of the room if I got lucky. You could kick him out of the room quick.

But Tommy Burleson was my favorite because of the basketball stuff we shared. Tommy didn't mind falling asleep with the TV on. Some guys wanted the TV off. But he didn't mind. We would both fall asleep with the TV on. I like to fall asleep with the TV on in hotels.

WORST ROOMMATE

The worst guy was Kennedy McIntosh. Kennedy didn't like that water too much, meaning he didn't like to shower. Kennedy was different. Kennedy talked a lot. He was spaced out. We used to say he was from the East Star. He is a piece of work.

COMEBACK

My second most memorable game occurred on January 31, 1975—a home game against Portland. We were at the Coliseum. Bill Walton was playing in Portland then, and we were down by 24 points with 16 minutes left to play.

Lenny Wilkens was in Portland, too. John Brisker was on our team. At the time, Brisker was in Russell's doghouse—what's new, right? I was coming off the bench, and the fans started chanting: "We want Slick! We want Slick!"

Russell broke down and put me in. He looked down the bench, and he and Brisker exchanged hard looks, but he put Brisker in, too. John ended up getting 18 points. I didn't get but about six, but what I did was pick up the tempo and started stealing the ball and diving everywhere.

In fact, Don Fair—always a big Slick fan—wrote:

"Watts, by rights, deserves the award for Leadership and Best Performance in a Supporting Role. What he didn't steal in the fourth quarter, he either popped loose or found the time to feed a teammate for a hoop. The bald-top one was near inhuman."

We came all the way back, and with the score tied at 102, there was a jump ball between Brisker and Walton. Bill had half a foot on Brisker. He tapped the ball toward his backcourt—but I was sneaky. I knew where Bill was going with the ball. When the ref threw it up, I ran toward where he was tapping the ball and got there first.

I missed the shot, but Fred Brown rebounded the ball, scored, and drew the foul. We won by three.

Man, that was a fun game.

SPAZZY RUSSELL

We were playing in L.A. about halfway through the season, and Cazzie Russell was a big-time superstar in his own mind because he could shoot the ball.

On this one play, he had a fast break, and I circled him and stripped the ball off his knee. I made a good play on him. I didn't jump on his back, but he told all the L.A. papers that I tried to hurt him intentionally.

The next time I went to L.A., they were ready for me at The Forum. I thought I was OJ Simpson. OJ hadn't been OJ yet, of course—but since I can make a comparison, I was OJ Simpson. Every newspaper story was about me, and they were all waiting for me.

However—Shine, Map Head—all those nicknames, they carried me through it all. In high school, I used to get those receptions. This time, 18,000 were waiting, and everything but a hammer was coming out of those stands.

I was playing. Lucius Allen would get it; Jerry West would get it; Gail Goodrich would get it; and I would say, "Give it here."

One writer wrote, "There was only one thing Slick Watts knew, and it was that a basketball was in the arena. And every time he got on the floor, he either stole it or scored it."

Jim Fox came up to me and said, "Are you human?"

"What do you mean?"

"I was so scared for you. Didn't they get to you?" he asked.

"I am from Rolling Fork, Mississippi, and in the places I played in high school, they didn't have no security. I just shut them out, and I was ballin'."

Cazzie is a Rick Barry-type of guy anyway, so now when I see him, I say hi and go. I know I didn't do anything wrong, so there was nothing to be straightened out. I picked his pocket.

LaRUE THE DAY

Big LaRue Martin blocked my shot in 1974-75. I think it was the only shot he blocked in his entire career. People still tease me about it.

LaRue was the first pick in the draft. He was the first player taken in the entire country, ahead of both Bob McAdoo and Julius Erving in 1972. Shows how much talent evaluators know what they're doing. I think LaRue had one good game against Bill Walton in the NCAA Tournament, and suddenly he was the top pick.

He was considered a failure in Portland. I thought I was becoming pretty good, and LaRue blocked my shot. He pinned my stuff right on the boards. People would come up to me and say, "Man, you ain't no good, LaRue blocked your stuff."

I will never forget that. It is true, too, because I have a picture of it. He has a picture of it, and I do too, but his is hanging over his fireplace because he had one block his whole career—on me.

SPENCER'S FALL FROM GRACE

The year 1974-75 ended up being Spencer Haywood's final season in Seattle—and it didn't end on a good note. He was the star; but, as I said before, Russell had the concept of team—and you don't run his team. He's the warden—he runs the prison; you don't.

Spencer started saying things about being disrespected, about not wanting to play in Seattle—he couldn't believe they would consider trading him. I remember when he used to come back to Seattle to play—it became a big soap opera.

Before he left, Spencer called me an "Uncle Tom." I don't know—I was starting to become popular at the time, so maybe he was jealous. I didn't mind him criticizing me. Maybe he was right, but at the time, I was just happy to be where I was. I wasn't worried about all that other stuff.

People wanted to give me $200 to eat steak and potatoes and come speak to their club? Why not? What else was I doing besides walking through the mall looking at pretty girls after practice?

If somebody was going to give me $200 to stop doing that and come make an appearance, then I was going to do it. I was caught up in the fun. Everywhere we went was fun. I wasn't caught up in the Spencer and Russ soap opera. It was a trip to be a part of something after coming from a small place and a small college where you had to watch UCLA and all the big schools playing in front of 20,000 people, when I had played in front of 500.

Spencer is such a good guy now. He is still an emotional guy—he still wants his props and thinks his number should be retired. You have to let that go.

Spencer, and Russell, too, for that matter, aren't the types to apologize. He never said he was sorry for calling me an Uncle Tom. Now Spencer will say stuff like, "Man, we are all grown up—we aren't tripping no more."

He said his family loves me. I think that is Spencer's way of apologizing.

Getting in the middle of the Bucks.
From the Donald Watts Collection

SUCCESS

Spencer's last year in Seattle happened to be the first time we experienced success—and when I say "we," I mean the entire Sonics organization.

Fred and I began to click. They brought in Leonard Gray. We went through the soap opera stuff with McDaniels and Brisker, and this was the first year we were over .500. Actually, the 1971-72 team was over .500, but this was the first winning team of which I had been a part.

The league was very balanced then—we didn't have as many teams, and each team had some superstars, so our record was above respectful. The team that beat us in the playoffs—the Golden State Warriors—won the championship, and we probably should have beaten them.

DETROIT

In the first round of the playoffs, we faced the Detroit Pistons. That would not have happened today since Detroit is in the East, but as I was saying, back then there were fewer teams.

Detroit had Bob Lanier—who had won the MVP award the year before—Curtis Rowe, Sidney Wicks, and Dave Bing, so they had the names on us. We had a better record and home-court advantage, but the Pistons had more experience and the big names. The team was a powerhouse.

I must say, I thought I was the key for us because I set the tempo. Each time they would bring me in, I was everywhere. Whenever I got in the game, Fred would pick up his play. I was going inside and kicking it out to Fred, and he was knocking down shots. We beat them in Game 1, lost in Game 2, and then beat them in Seattle in Game 3 to win the series. We shouldn't have beaten them, but we did.

GOLDEN STATE

Rick Barry went crazy on us. I remember there were many fights in the series. Leonard Gray and Rick Barry—boy, they used to hook up. Leonard was our enforcer, so he would bump Rick and try to make him cry. Fans poured beer all over Rick when he was coming through the tunnel. Rick was mad—he went after the fans, and the police grabbed Rick. It was a big thing. Leonard wanted us to let him loose. Leonard wanted to go over and kick Rick's butt.

Rick is a Hall of Famer, and nobody even knows who Leonard Gray is—but Leonard could play. Yet, if you had a different philosophy than the coach's, you were gone. Believe me: I know that. I didn't know it then, but I know it now. I learned the hard way. It's too bad, too, because Leonard could play. Leonard had Rick strung out there for a while, but Rick was a hard-nosed fighter—he and Clifford Ray got us.

In Game 6, I was the leading scorer, but we lost that game and the series, 4-2. Russell said after that game: "Slick did everything he could to win that game by himself. That was one of the greatest games I have ever seen by a player."

The other guys didn't come to play. I scored 24 points, dished 11 assists, and grabbed five steals that night. I came to win, but the other guys just froze—they kind of choked on me. All our so-called "big scorers" disappeared.

I thought we would have beaten the Washington Bullets if we had gotten to them in the Finals—Rick and Golden State swept them four straight. The Bullets were 50-32, and they were swept. They were iced. We lost to the Warriors in six.

In the end, I think it was just a combination of too much soap opera and too much of the Big Fella. He intimidated our shooters to the point where they didn't bring their lunch pails.

CHAPTER 6

1975-76

THE LEAGUE

The biggest difference between the game then and the game now is television coverage. We had great crowds most places, but we weren't on TV. In other cities, however—like Buffalo—one dribble would echo for an hour. There was no energy in Buffalo—just empty red seats—having a franchise in that city never made sense to me.

Los Angeles was always a good place to play. Oakland—when Golden State had Rick Barry—always filled it up. Pete Maravich in New Orleans—he used to draw crowds. All those guys in Atlanta, all the sisters and brothers would come out there. Atlanta is a dead zone today, but back then it was a good spot. In the Red Holzman years, Walt Frazier and Earl Monroe were great.

New Jersey was blah. Everybody hated New Jersey. We always stayed in New York when we played there. The janitor would never get up to turn on the heat, so you froze in the building. It was definitely not a player's place to play; you didn't feel like fighting.

And I have to say: I was disappointed with the Boston Celtics, too. It's funny—all you used to watch on TV was Bill Russell and Wilt Chamberlain play on those beautiful boards. Then you would get there and the ball would kick up into the stands. Russ used to tell me that Red did that on purpose.

Another famous Auerbach story Russ used to share was how Red made the nets bigger. The maintenance man always made sure the nets were bigger so that when you'd shoot it through, the ball would come out quickly, and Russ would step out and start a fast break.

"Even on the makes we could start a fast break, Slick," Russ would say. "Ack, ack, ack . . . because the nets were big." He used to tell me that story about the nets a lot.

Red was always thinking. Big Fella was getting all this stuff from Red. And I thought the rim and nets actually were bigger— or at least it seemed like they were. Maybe Big Russ put it in my head, but the rims in Boston always felt like they were bigger. They said I wasn't a shooter, but I always shot well in Boston because the rims felt bigger. I used to love the Boston rims.

Cleveland had the tightest rims—I hated those rims. You know how some golf course holes seem like they are smaller than others and some feel like they are bigger than others? They are probably the same size, but for some reason, I guess the maintenance keeps the greens so nice you have to putt them true. In Cleveland, you really had to swish the shot. Unlike Boston, you could never catch a bounce. That's probably why the Celtics won all those championships.

FIRST FAVORITE GAME

We were playing the Detroit Pistons on February 15, 1976. After this game, a singer named Jim Tate made a song about it called, "Slick is his name, let him play his game." The song was about this game. When I go to the store or church or speaking engagements, people always ask, "Slick, do you remember that game?"

We were down six points with 34 seconds to go. Russ called timeout and tried to give instructions. I looked up in the stands and people were walking to the parking lot.

They should have stayed.

First, Bob Lanier fouls Herm Gilliam, who hit two free throws. Then I stole the ball on a George Trapp pass, and we scored again—so we were down by two.

Then Archie Clark got the ball. I knocked it from Archie off the referee. Archie looked at the ref, so I dove over him and got the ball. I passed ahead to Big Tommy Burleson, who dunked it with 16 seconds left to tie the game. What was left of the crowd was going crazy.

Detroit came down again. Curtis Rowe drove to the basket and scored, but I drew an offensive foul on him, and the basket was waved off—timeout with three seconds to go.

Everybody was quiet. Russell said: "Slick, I want you to bring it in. Leonard, I want you to set a pick for Fred. And Fred, I want you to shoot it."

"Sorry, Coach, no sir, why don't we try something freaky and give the ball to me?" I told him. "I'm going to shoot."

"What did I just say?" Russ snapped back. "Don't talk back to me, boy. I will take you out of the game."

"No sir, I am shooting it," I assured him. Here I had made the big plays and brought us all the way back, and he wanted Fred to shoot it?

I said it again: "I'm shooting it."

"Get on out of here," he told me. He wanted me to sit down, but I stayed in the game.

Leonard set that pick for Fred, and everybody froze. Everybody froze. It was almost as if time stood still. Nobody wanted to shoot it. I broke out of a pack of players, almost at the center line, got the ball, threw it up toward the basket from 30 feet, and it looked like the wind just blew it in.

After the game, Burleson told the *Seattle Times*: "I thought Slick's shot would miss by a mile. But I won't doubt it next time."

The headline in the *Seattle Post-Intelligencer* read: "Watt(s) a Miracle!" That bad boy looked like it curved in, but it was nothing but net. The fans were jumping and hollering. Boy, that was an exciting game. Bob Blackburn was going crazy on the radio.

From there, we began to play well, and we made the playoffs. In fact, that game catapulted us to a franchise-record eight-game win streak.

A DIFFERENT KIND OF NBA RECORD

After that game, Jim Tate, an old country singer who loved basketball, wrote a song about the game. It's called "Slick is his name; Let him play his game."

It goes something like this:
There were three seconds left
For playing ball
The score was tied,
107 all
Time was out,
They slowed the pace
Fans were starting
To leave the place
Slick is his name
Let him play his game
Let him play his game
Time out Circle, the mood is good
Just trying to figure out what to do
Not one player made a sound
They thought they were overtime bound

Slick is his name
Let him play his game
Let him play his game
A voice was heard
From out of the blue
'I feel kind of freaky
Let me shoot the 2'
When they saw who it was that spoke
The guys thought Slick was making a joke
Slick is his name
Let him play his game
Let him play his game
Someone said, 'Are you for real?
Do you think you can shoot as well as steal?'
Slick just gave a knowing wink
He believed that he could make it sink
Slick is his name
Let him play his game
Let him play his game
The guys agreed they had nothing to lose
So they let Slick start, he had paid his dues
They said, 'Hey Coach, we heard enough,
Inbound to Slick and let him try his stuff'
Slick is his name
Let him play his game
Let him play his game
They clapped their hands and they took their place
Only Slick had a smiling face
The fans who stayed were as hot as could be
They all were standing and trying to see
Slick is his name
Let him play his game
Let him play his game
Now the time was up and the time was in
They all were awaiting for the play to begin

Slick made his play, he moved inside
He called for the pass and let it ride
Slick is his name
Let him play his game
Let him play his game
When he let it ride you could see it was 2
He said to the guys, 'I did it for you'
The fans were jumping and stomping like mad
They really dig this slick-haired lad
Slick is his name
Let him play his game
Let him play his game
They were jumping and a stomping in broad daylight
Jumping and a stomping in broad daylight
Well they were jumping and a stomping
In a broad daylight
Yes they were
They were jumping and a stomping
They were jumping and a stomping
Jumping and stomping

He wrote it in 1975-76, and he was getting ready to put it out in '77. The local radio stations agreed to play it, and then Little Fella—Lenny—came to town.

Just before they started to put out the song, I was on a plane—I'd been traded. Nobody ever heard the song, but Jim Tate sent me a little 45 of it that I still have.

DUNK YOU VERY MUCH

One night against the Detroit Pistons, I got a lay-up. I didn't dunk it, but I actually got my wrist over the rim and kind of cute-dunked it. After the game, I was on the radio show with Bob Blackburn. He used to give each of us a $15 gift certificate to be on the talk show after the game—I was excited about that $15.

Anyway, Bob says to me: "That looked like a little dunk. But you can't really dunk."

And I said, "Look, man, I can dunk."

He kept egging me on, saying, "Slick Watts says he can dunk, but I don't think he can really dunk."

I had gotten about 28 that night, and I was feeling good—I was on a high. I pulled out a chair, and he said, "You are going to need a ladder. What are you going to do, stand up on the chair?"

"No, I am going to jump over this chair and dunk."

I put the chair in front of the goal and took a running start from the top of the key. This was during the interview, mind you—Bob still had on his headphones. I picked that bad boy up, tucked it in my hands, and threw it down.

The look on his face was precious—they'd never seen me dunk before that, I'm sure of it. With Russ breathing over me, had I missed a dunk in a game, he'd have benched my little ol' butt for a month. Fred could dunk, but he never messed with it—he just finger rolled.

Blackburn signed off with this:

"That was the only time Slick ever dunked the ball. I just wanted to make sure that he could do it because I always told him—in jest, but in reality—that if he couldn't, I would get a stepladder out so he could go up and do it. I can't tell you why he never did it in games because Slick knows what show business is all about, and basketball is show business just like anything else. That was why he was such a lovely character."

NATIONAL RECOGNITION

After that comeback against Detroit, people started to take notice of me. *Sport* Magazine sent a writer up from San Francisco, and he wrote an article that said, "Slick Watts towers over Bill Russell."

It was talking about Sam Schulman hiring Bill Russell, and how a little guy from Mississippi came out of nowhere and he was the guy people in Seattle were coming to see.

An excerpt of the story, written by Ralph Barbieri, states:

"Bill Russell is still the coach and general manager of the Seattle SuperSonics, but the Sonics no longer sell tickets on his name and reputation. The Sonics sell more tickets now. They sell them on Slick Watts's name and reputation. In Seattle, Slick Watts not only towers over Bill Russell; he's bigger than Puget Sound. He's the most popular athlete in the history of the state. He's the most famous unknown who ever lived."

Lord, when I boarded the plane after that, there was no more, "Boy, come sit on up here." Daddy put me on ice for a week or two.

"Coach, I don't even know the writer's name," I tried to tell him. "He came to my house and rode in my car for four days."

But what happened was, as he rode around with me, people would see me, and strange things would happen. I am not kidding—just out-of-this-world things.

I was sitting at a traffic light, and some kids recognized me so they asked me for my autograph. Then somebody else recognized me, and he came over. Then everybody started getting out of their cars, and there was a traffic jam around my car because everybody wanted my autograph.

That same week, there was a traffic accident in downtown Seattle—just a little fender bender, nothing serious. The people got out of their cars and started yelling at each other. So I got out of my car and tried to help. That's how I was; I liked to help people. However, the two people arguing recognized me, and all of a sudden, everything was okay. They got some autographs from me, exchanged information, and the whole thing was resolved.

Barbieri wrote all that stuff. Just driving around town, he saw people react to me, and he couldn't believe it. He wrote the truth, but it was scary. Unbelievable.

Avoiding Bill Walton was no easy task.
From the Donald Watts Collection

Then *Sports Illustrated* came to town and did a big ol' story on me. They talked about how big I was and how I could be governor of the state of Washington.

In that story, John Papanek wrote:

"Whether or not Slick Watts is the most popular athlete ever to perform in the state of Washington is no longer in question. Forget Hugh McElhenny, Elgin Baylor, and Lenny Wilkens. The question now is: Why do Washingtonians regard a totally bald, six-foot, 24-year-old, black backcourt man as the most popular person ever to live in the state?"

All the guys kind of gave me a cold shoulder after that.

GOING BIG TIME

After those stories came out, I got stupid and bought a Mercedes. I had a nice orange Volkswagen that I bought my rookie year once I made the team. Everybody loved Slick in the orange VW.

I used to drive to my speaking engagements. I was the man the Sonics sent around to do all the promotions for community events. I went to Yakima, Spokane, everywhere. I would do it in that little VW—everybody knew that little VW.

But then I tried to be like the big-timers. I went out and got a Mercedes. A little two-seat Mercedes from Phil Smart. Matter of fact, Spencer Haywood ordered it, but he was too big to get into it, so it was like a hand-me-down for me. I picked it up, trying to be cool.

After that, the guys started looking at me differently. Russell even asked me, "Boy, what are you doing with that car?" Back then, they wanted you to stay in your place.

Russell said, "You got a big head, boy."

I said, "I'm not keeping that car, it's a user."

That got him off me for a little bit—long enough for me to go out and buy a little Volvo.

From that point on, I left the Mercedes in my garage.

BANDITRY

Toward the end of this season, I was leading the league in steals and actually set the single-season NBA steals record—and I did it with 11 games still left to play in the season.

The day before I set the record, I tied Rick Barry's mark of 228 by grabbing five steals in a game against the Rockets. You know Rick didn't feel good about it—he didn't want anybody taking his records—but I was proud of it. After that game, Houston coach John Egan told the *Seattle Times*: "With eight rebounds, seven assists, five steals, 23 points, he completely annihilated us."

As I watch today's game, the guys don't come up and challenge people as we did. I guess it takes a lot of hard work. Nobody really challenges the ball-handler and tries to close him out in a full-court situation. Everybody tries to play the passing lanes. I know they say that it's because the athletes are so good now—but I think it is laziness.

I used to challenge. I used to know how to play a ball-handler's weakness. Watching a guy like Lenny Wilkens—who likes to use his left hand—I would fake to the left and go back to the right.

I was real sneaky quick. I used to like to go behind the center after he was concentrating on beating his man, and I would sneak in, poke it out real quick, and get away before he could knock me out with those big old elbows.

Two nights after tying Rick's record, I was playing the Suns in Phoenix when I broke the record. It was a good feeling when the game concluded. When I broke it, Rick Welts—who is a vice president with the Suns now, but was up-and-coming with the Sonics then—affirmed: "Shine, you did it, you got the steals record."

My theory about why I was so good defensively—it was my quickness. I was always the smallest guy on the basketball court. And so my theory was that, since I was shorter, it usually took the thoughts in my brain a shorter amount of time to reach my hands and feet than it did somebody who was taller, because with somebody taller it had farther to travel.

Besides Randy Smith, I felt I was the quickest, fastest player in the league. I once told Don Fair: "I think I have the quickest hands in the West. Sometimes I stand up before a mirror and flick at myself to see how quick I am, and I have a time keeping up with myself—sometimes."

MR. COMMUNITY

In 1975-76 I won the NBA's Citizenship Award. This was a good year for me, to say the least—the best year of my life.

The NBA requires its players to go to two or three community-related events a year. Hospitals, or speaking engagements, or schools, whatever is needed to get out in the community, mingle with the people.

That year, I went to 300 events—almost one a day. But remember: We were often on the road, so what that really meant was, sometimes I went to several a day.

One day I was at the supermarket, and a lady asked me to go to her son's birthday party. I had a doctor's appointment or something, and so I said no, but she kept asking. So I just left the store and went to her son's birthday party—I skipped my doctor's appointment. That was cool. The kids loved me, and I loved them.

Some guys didn't like to do the community events, but I loved them. Man, I came from nowhere. The only things people knew me for were my bald head and headband. I was the freak. Now that people loved me and wanted to be around me—I wanted to be around them, too. That was part of the reason I became so popular, because I was a so-called superstar who could relate to

SLICK WATTS assignments

January

8	J.C.Penneys SouthCenter	3-5
8	The Family House	7-
10	MAN OF THE YEAR BANQUET	7
11	Cottage Lake Elem	1-3:30
11	*Family House*	*5:30*
12	Sharples Jr. Hi	1:30-*2:30*
15	J.C.Penneys Tacoma Mall	3-5
18	Loyal Heights School	7-
22	*OUT OF TOWN* ~~J.C.Penneys Northgate~~	~~3-5~~
29	J.C.Penneys Downtown	3-5
29	Queen Anne Lutheran Church	6-

SEATTLE SUPERSONICS

221 W. HARRISON ST.
SEATTLE, WA 98119

One of Slick's monthly community service schedules.
From the Donald Watts Collection

them—who wasn't too big to come to your house for a birthday party.

I have to admit, the one thing I feel badly about is that I would sometimes miss appointments. What happened is, I would commit to attend too many events, and they would overlap, so I couldn't make both at the same time.

But it wasn't because I was big-timing them. It was because I was out seeing other people.

NOT-SO-FREE THROW

Over the course of my career, I was a 60-percent free-throw shooter, and I would like to think it was because my defense was so good.

I would say with all honesty that I really feel that the great shooters don't play any defense. When I was in high school, I didn't play much defense. Then when I got to the NBA and it was do or die, I played defense so hard that when I got to the free-throw line, I rested instead of concentrating on shooting the free throws.

Now I can stand up and hit 100 straight free throws. But if I had to harass you down the court 10 or 12 times, get up on you all the way up and down the court, it took it out of me—it takes it out of your concentration. I really believe I overplayed myself. When I got to the free throw line, I was so happy just to rest.

To me, every possession was my last, because the most strenuous situation in the world was to play under Bill Russell. You always had a big hammer over your head, and it could fall at any given time. You could never relax. Russell could always put the hook on you. When I got to the line, my body was overcoming my hyperactivity.

My free throw shooting did become an issue. It was like a bad marriage—I can't live with him, and I can't live without him. I would put the tempo up, and we would be winning. But then, in

Slick at a precarious place: the free throw line.
From the Donald Watts Collection

the last four minutes, sometimes I had to sit. At least I understood why.

KING FOR A DAY—OR DAYS

Because I was so popular at the time, they invited me to be a
special guest at the opening of the Kingdome. The mayor was
there, some state senators, and the governor. Everybody was
there.

They introduced all those guys, and they received some
applause, just polite applause. And then they called my name,
and you couldn't hear anything but "Slick, Slick, Slick" chanted
by like 50,000 or 60,000 people. I got a five-minute standing
ovation, just standing there being cheered by that many people.
That was one of the most chilling feelings a human being can
have.

It was as if I were the first legitimate, genuine sports figure to
which people attached themselves. Spencer had been here, but he
was untouchable. Russell was there, but they were scared of him.
I was a rags-to-riches story. I was happy-go-lucky. They could
relate to me, so it was an astounding feeling to come from
nowhere and then to feel that.

I used to go to the store in Mississippi, and they would won-
der if I was stealing something. Then I'd go to the store in Seattle,
and everybody was just amazed that I was there—pointing, talking about me, asking for autographs.

I felt like the Beatles for a hot minute. I had to move twice.
After games, people were sitting around my house with posters. I
was in Kirkland on Bridle Trail. My wife finally said, "We have to
move. I can't take this anymore."

Then they named me the SeaFair Grand Marshall. Bob Hope
was once a SeaFair Grand Marshall. All this was just coming
down on a little ol' boy from Rolling Fork, Mississippi. Actually,
I was named Grand Marshall twice. The first time, I didn't really

Ready to set sail in style.
From the Donald Watts Collection

know what it was, so I showed up in jeans and a t-shirt. But the second time, I realized what a big deal it was, so I showed up in a nice suit, looking clean.

What I was doing, though—and at the time I didn't know it—but I was creating enemies with that because it was putting me on a different level. I was like George Jefferson—*moving on up*. However, I didn't understand that yet. I was still enjoying it.

I went from that boy who was getting sandwiches for everybody in New York to somebody who everybody gets quiet around and acts like you are special. It was a very strange feeling.

JUMPING ON THE BANDWAGON

I got to be so popular that other folks started trying to cash in on my popularity.

One night I had a party at my house in Bellevue for Senator Warren Magnusson. He was a senator for 44 years. He was the longest-term senator ever in the state of Washington. It was a fund-raising party just to help him with his reelection.

He was about 89 years old, and they were trying to boot him out of the senate. All the politicians were there at my house. He was so old that he couldn't even walk up my steps. I had a big old mansion then, and we had to nearly carry him up the stairs.

NEW CONTRACT

Toward the end of the 1975-76 season, the Sonics decided to renegotiate my contract before the start of the next season.

After all, this is what Bob Walsh, our general manager, told *Sports Illustrated*:

"It's impossible to calculate Slick's worth to the team. He puts at least 1,000 a night into the Coliseum, and those are just the people he's met in the past week or kids he's met who demand

Slick with former U.S. Senator Warren Magnusson.
From the Donald Watts Collection

that their parents take them to the game. Even if he couldn't play, he'd be worth an awful lot to us. If we ever traded him, we'd all have to leave town."

I had hired Bob Mussehl to be my agent. All the other big-timers had Mussehl, so I wanted to get a big-time agent, too. I figured that if he could get all those jokers that big money, he could get me the same thing.

The first time Bob went in to talk with Big Fella, Russ didn't even discuss the contract. Bob was in this meeting with Russell for five hours, and all Russell did was talk about his championships.

Bob called me and said, "Slick, he didn't even bring you up. All he did was talk about his past achievements."

And I said, "That's the Big Fella."

Here I was paying my lawyer about $250 an hour—so it cost me over $1,000 for him to hear about Russell's glory days.

When they finally did start discussing money, I asked for a five-year deal starting at $120,000 and topping out at $176,000. Spencer had been making $302,000. Big Tommy was getting $325,000. Even Frank Oleynick, who played sparingly, was getting $100,000.

The Sonics offered a three-year deal that started at $70,000, that escalated $10,000 per year. I accepted.

Want to know why I accepted? Russell. He strong-armed me. The Big Fella's own insecurities hurt me.

Russell told me: "Boy, it took me ten years to make $100,000. Wilt Chamberlain has $100,000. And I have $100,001. Ack, ack, ack, ack, ack . . . I'm not giving you that type of goddamn money. It took me 10 years."

It didn't matter to him that all these other guys were being paid—even unproven guys. I just think that he couldn't accept that a guy he discovered—an undrafted guy who came out of nowhere and all of a sudden had a bigger name in the city than he did—was going to make more money than he did as a player. Big Fella could laugh off the magazine stories about us, but he couldn't be the one to pay me more money than he ever made.

So he told me this: "Before I leave, I promise you this, Slick. I will get you $1 million."

And then the next year, he was gone—that was the one downfall of my career.

THINGS HAPPEN FOR A REASON

It's probably just as well I didn't make a ton of money when I was playing. If I had the kind of money they make today, I would probably have had a heart attack.

One time, I thought I had won the lottery. I was in Fall City. I had an $11 million ticket. I looked at it, and my chest started pounding. I got nervous. My head became feverish. Man, I thought I had won $11 million, and I didn't know how to handle it.

As it turned out, the ticket had expired. It was the same number, but on a different day. I told my wife that I was glad I didn't win that money because sometimes money can kill you.

But had I won that money, I would have called the Department of Transportation and told them I'd give them $100,000 to make sure nobody was on the road between Seattle and Olympia. I wouldn't want to take any chances of anybody getting in an accident with me. Then my newly purchased limousine would have taken me down to Olympia where I'd pick up my winnings.

THE END OF THE ROAD

I didn't know it at the time, but this was the last time I would play a playoff game for the Sonics. We ended the year 43-39—the exact same record as the year before. We drew Phoenix in the first round of the playoffs.

John MacLeod was the Suns coach. They had Paul Westphal and Alvin Adams. I hoped we would've done better in the playoffs, particularly since I had such a good year individually—but I thought Alvin Adams was very impressive with his outside shot, bringing our big men away from the basket.

I mostly guarded Westphal. He wasn't too quick, but he was very deliberate and understood the game. He knew how to post you up, put you on his hip, and he had a good swing-in move. He made you fight him hard because he was considered a big guard. He didn't talk a lot of trash—he just went to work. He was one of the better players in the league at that time—he and Charley Scott, their other guard.

We ended up losing the series four games to two. I had some bitter memories of that too; I wish I had shot some free throws better. I thought I had a decent playoff series as far as setting the team up, but I thought Westphal worked me so hard that I missed some key free throws that I thought I should have made. I didn't like that—I felt as if I hurt the team.

CHAPTER 7

FAME

Sometimes professional athletes are lucky and become popular—some become superstars—and you get chances for things to happen for you, or you get opportunities to meet truly famous people who make history. You go into shock when you meet someone famous—I know. You go home and call all your friends and family to tell them whom you met. Fortunately, I was able to call my friends and family often.

I learned something important once I became the top sports personality in Seattle: No. 1 athletes from other cities want to hang out with the No. 1 athlete in the cities they visit. Since I was "The Man" in Seattle, those guys would look me up and ask me to show them the city.

As a result of this rule, I—a little ol' boy from Rolling Fork, Mississippi—met and became friends with some of the greatest figures of all time.

WILT

Wilt was a ladies man, and he liked himself. Not only did he enjoy being big, he actually had a reason for his ego. However, he also knew how to level with you and make you feel good around him. He didn't smother you with his pride all the time.

He would say things and try to slap me five, and I would have a complex because my hand was so small. When I slapped him five, it was like a baby's hand in his hand. Yet, he was softer and kinder to be around than Russell was.

NIGHTS WITH WILT

I hung out with Wilt when I was playing, and we remained friends even after I retired. Every night that I went out with him, it was as if I was working. He would call and say that he was coming, and we'd meet at the Sheraton hotel in downtown Seattle.

I had a Mercedes 450-SC. I had moved up in the world. But that didn't help Wilt—he was still too big. I would pull up in my Benz, and his limo would wait out in front. Then I'd pull my Benz in behind his limo. We had it going on now—I knew how to stage it.

We had drinks at the Saratoga Trunk in Bellevue. Wilt was the best—he was so tall that when we went places, I would insist that he sit down and I stand up, and then we would both be the same height, and he would, because he was a nice guy.

I don't know why people thought I was like his bodyguard, but they would come up to me and ask, "Can I speak to Wilt? Can I meet Wilt?"

He would say, "Tell her where I'm staying." Then when we got back to the hotel, it was like another game—it was on.

TRUTH OR FICTION?

I read Wilt's book, and he didn't sleep with 25,000 women. But this is the truth—I know he would meet 1,000 women in a night. They would go after him like flies on honey. They would just come up and introduce themselves—God's honest truth. Those stories you read about him and how the ladies reacted— they are all true.

After we got back from the Saratoga Trunk, all the women he had invited back from the bar lined up outside his room. He had a suite at the Sheraton, so he would sit in the front room, and the girls would be out in the hallway. They would come in the room one by one.

And he was like, "Come on in. Turn around."

He'd look at them. If they passed his examination, he'd say, "Go sit in that room." They'd go sit in the other room and wait for him.

If they weren't hot enough, he'd say, "Slick, tell her to get out of here."

He would actually look at them and say, "You are not nice enough to hang out with me."

But it didn't matter—women were so excited to meet him they would actually follow him to a room like they were dogs and he had treats.

Now after they went into the other room, I don't know what he did with them. I ain't going to act like I was in the room, but I know he had the room, and they would come through just to be in his presence. I know he had his choice.

Wilt had some good times.

MISCOMMUNICATION

After I retired, I was a food broker. I was still friends with Wilt, though, and we still hung out when he came to town.

My boss's wife, a real short woman, she loved Wilt Chamberlain. My boss was what I called "Celebrified"—he liked to know and meet a lot of celebrities. So I worked the angle—when I brought my boss and his wife to meet Mr. So-and-So Celebrity, my paycheck went up a little bit.

So I called my boss's wife one day and said, "I'm with Wilt Chamberlain."

And she said, "Please . . . I want to meet him. I have to meet him."

So I said to Wilt, "Wilt, my boss's wife wants to meet you."

Much like Russell, however, Wilt's ego was so huge that he thought when a woman wants to meet you, it meant sex—she wants some of the "Stilt."

Nonetheless, I arranged for them to meet. When I told Wilt she had arrived, he said, "Bring her up."

She came into the room, but when she did, he looked at her and said, "Get her out of here."

She didn't look good enough for him—and she just wanted an autograph. Man, she was so crushed. She asked, "Why did he tell me to get out of there?"

I played it off. "Well, Wilt, he's moody."

I didn't tell her she wasn't good enough for him. When I see her at the mall now, I have to laugh about that day.

WILT AND RUSSELL

I must admit, as much talking as he did, Russell wouldn't talk to me too much about himself. Russ wouldn't share too many stories about Wilt. Russ mostly shared stories about Red Auerbach.

Wilt would say to me, "They try to make stories about us, but we go to dinner sometimes. We respect each other."

Wilt would talk about Russell, and said that they had no disagreements about who was the best center and whatnot—the press just liked to portray it that way.

However, they did have a rivalry. Back in those days, that's all they showed on television—Wilt Chamberlain versus Bill Russell. It was almost like there were only two teams in the league. In the years that Boston won eight or nine championships, Wilt was the only man who challenged Russell.

Every year, something bad happened to him. He hurt his knee—then Russell would make a statement about how he'd play on one leg if it were him. The press would blow the story up, but Wilt actually told me he had no problem with it.

My personal feeling is: Russ was a winner because he won with a better team—but as far as skill, nobody has had as much skill as Wilt Chamberlain. Wilt was the most skillful center who ever played the game.

RUSSELL'S FAVORITE WILT STORY

This was the one story Russell used to tell me about Wilt— and he told it often. Russ did so much talking that I think he forgot who he told stories to, so many times he would repeat them.

He told me this story about a hundred times, and he loved it so much, he'd cackle before he even told it.

"Ack, ack, ack. Slick," he'd say, "I remember when I used to be getting ready to play Chamberlain. Chamberlain had dunked on everybody. And Red asked me, 'You going to let him keep dunking on you?' So I went back into the game, Wilt got ready to dunk, and I took off running. Wilt was so surprised that he dropped the ball and yelled, 'Hey Russ, where you going?'"

Then Russell would look at you and say, "I stopped him, didn't I? Ack, ack, ack."

MOSES MALONE

Big Mo. Moses was my man. I got a big picture of Moses and me together. I called him Mo because he used to say we would "win in fo'."

Mo was a young guy then. He had played with Utah and then transferred to the NBA. He was with Houston and I was with Seattle. Whenever he came to town, we used to hook up and hang at "Sundays."

When I was traded to Houston, Mo had this gigantic mansion—a very beautiful home—swimming pool, big backyard, everything. I had this hole-in-the-wall apartment.

You know where we used to spend our time? That's right—the hole-in-the-wall apartment.

And I'd say, "Mo, you got this $4 million home. Why can't we go to your house?"

I went to his house one time in a year and a half—one time. He came to my house 1,000 times. I think I was an outlet. He was married with children—I think I made him feel young and alive. But I could never understand it. We could have been laying by the swimming pool drinking mai-tais in a Hawaiian setting. But no—we were in my tiny apartment by the Galleria mall.

Every day we played checkers. Every damn day. He loved checkers. He tried to jump you five or six times. If you beat him, he wouldn't let you move. He was a big fella, so I stayed put when he said, "Come on, man, we got to play again."

GOING TO THE TRACK

If Mo and I weren't playing checkers, we'd go down to the University of Houston—where Carl Lewis went to school—and we would watch him run. We would talk to Carl a little bit, but he was real young. He was like 17. He knew who we were, but he never did hang with us, because he knew we were up to no good.

Slick with his main man, Big Mo.
From the Donald Watts Collection

I had my 1976 Mercedes Benz then, and Mo had a Rolls Royce. We both thought we were cool, so we would park the cars behind each other. He would park the Rolls, and then I would park the Benz ten yards behind him with the top down. We were so stupid, but we thought we were cool.

Then we would get out and sit on the hoods of our cars. We used to watch Carl—but you know what we were doing? At the University of Houston, pretty girls would stroll by, so we would girl watch. We would do that three or four times a week, and in between that, we'd go play checkers.

Mo . . . that was my boy.

BOB LANIER

Because I still wasn't making a lot of money, I used to have this little orange Volkswagen that I would ride around Seattle in. Man, everybody knew that little orange Volkswagen. I would drive around and people would wave to me all day, "Yo, Slick, what's going on?"

The problem was, all these big-name guys came to town and they were looking for Slick Watts because I was the man at the time, and they were expecting a limo to show up. Instead, I'd show up in my little orange Volkswagen.

Bob Lanier came to town, and he rode around in my Volkswagen. "Man, you Slick Watts! What you doing riding around in this little Volkswagen?"

I'll never forget that—Bob Lanier, with his big old 22s, riding in an orange Volkswagen. He almost got stuck in the car.

I told him, covering the truth: "Man, this is my little fake car. Yeah, I got to get me another car."

Showing off a little 1970s fashion.
From the Donald Watts Collection

"SUNDAYS"

When all these fellas came into town, I usually took them to a place called "Sundays." I would take Wilt over to Bellevue, but just about everybody else—I took to Sundays.

Sundays was an old converted church on the corner of Mercer and First Avenue in lower Queen Anne. It has been torn down since and is now a local market, but back in the day that was the spot.

Sundays was the spot for super-brothers. Not just black—super-black. If you made over fifty grand . . . man, they had beautiful women in there.

We'd go in there to hang out and play backgammon.

STUDIO 54

I made it into Studio 54 three times when I went to New York. It was THE place—if you got in there, you were part of the establishment.

I didn't think I was big time enough to get in. At the time, I still hadn't accepted that I was part of this so-called cool structure. I went there fully expecting to be rejected, but people on the east coast knew my headband—so I got in. When people embraced me, it made me feel like the mayor.

Studio 54 was just lights, music, pictures on the wall—almost like a scene out of the movies. Everybody is somebody, and every one is wearing a mink coat. Everybody is dressed to impress. In an entire evening, you'd never be able to eye all the famous people there.

My head was shining, and I thought I was clean—tons of fun, excitement, ladies, and other hip people.

Man, you really thought you had arrived when you could get in there.

THE BROWN BOMBER

Joe Frazier was in Studio 54 one time when I was there. I talked to Joe about the big fight he had fought with Muhammad Ali in New York—the one at Madison Square Garden that enthusiasts called the fight of the century.

That was the fight when Frazier had sent Ali to the deck with that big left hook. Joe told me about that left hook through his strained voice while he was wearing a big old red suit with a huge red hat. He talked about how he danced, and moved, and hit him with the left hook.

At that time, he was sensitive about Ali, because Ali had said a bunch of stuff about him. Frazier told me, "I made him, I made Ali."

I don't want to talk bad about Joe—Joe is a nice guy—but to me he always looked like he didn't know where he was. He seemed like he was ducking and jabbing while he was talking to you. He spoke very fast, and he rambled. He bobbed and weaved when he talked to you.

Boxers get hit a lot—and I think Joe got hit even more.

DIANA ROSS

Diana Ross was in Studio 54 another time I was there. I wanted to get to her and talk to her about some things, but she had too many big people around her. I think she invented the word "bodyguards."

JESSE JACKSON

Jesse was a character. Back in the '70s, he was coming to preach at the AME church and Mt. Zion when he came to

Seattle. I used to go to church, especially when he was in town, and I used to try to donate money to his causes.

Man, Jesse would call you out. You'd be in church, and, trying to raise money for whatever, he'd bellow, "Slick Watts, come up here. Give me $1,000."

And he would look at your check, too—he would call you out. He'd say, "This guy is playing ball, and he only gives $100." But I wasn't making any money then, so I didn't appreciate that much.

But Jesse, he knew how to work it. He always liked press and wanted to become known even before he became the prominent figure he is today. So he would always hook up with the top athlete in each town, and that is how he would get good press.

I was cooking then, so we'd hook up, and he would go down to the Kingdome with me. That way, when we walked through, because he was with me, everybody in Seattle would know he was Jesse Jackson, not just some angry brother.

I knew what he was up to, but for me he was just fun to be around because he was one of these untouchable brothers—I thought he was going to be the next Martin Luther King.

It was another one of those things where I was a nobody coming from nowhere, so he helped lift my spirits and gave me a little more sense of self-worth.

REGGIE JACKSON

When Reggie came to town, he called up the Sonics' offices one day and got my phone number. Even though we played different sports, The Man in one town wants to hang with The Man in the other town.

I got some tickets and went down to the Kingdome to watch Reggie's game. I remember, when I walked in and pulled off my hat, the music stopped. For that brief time, when I walked in, I was like Mike or Ali. After the game, I took Reggie to "Sundays," and we'd have drinks and play backgammon.

PRESIDENT JIMMY CARTER

In 1976, I led the league in assists and steals. President Carter was coming to Seattle, so I was chosen to help greet him at Boeing Field. I was the fourth guy to welcome him off the plane. The top three were the governor, a senator, and the mayor. I was next in line.

I look at all that stuff like Edgar Martinez meeting President Bush down at Boeing Field, and I smile. Edgar played in Seattle for 18 years to do that. I did it in less than five.

Carter has a good heart. He is a good ol' Georgia Boy. He actually called me Slick. He actually remembered me from my college playing days. That was another uplifting event for a small ego.

We talked about basketball. He said I was a good little player—he liked the way I hustled. He said his mother was a big fan of mine. That was about it, but it made me feel important.

TED TURNER

I think the league changed when cable TV came into play. I think cable was crucial to the league. Ted Turner starting cable TV and bringing in CNN news was the most instrumental factor of the league's appeal today.

The league itself credits Larry Bird and Magic Johnson playing in the national championship in college and then coming into the league together for igniting the NBA's popularity. I think that revived the league, but they were just two people. They did boost the ratings on some level when they played each other, but they still had to be seen.

That is why I thought Ted Turner was more instrumental in turning things around. Before that, there were only three stations, and it seemed like the only games aired were when Wilt faced Russ. Ted helped everybody get exposure, and that helped the league grow.

He actually came to try to get us to invest with him in cable TV. Like the dummies that we were, we thought CBS, NBC and ABC weren't going to let that happen.

We also thought cable TV was like Amway. Amway made a lot of money but everybody got tired of being approached by them and hearing: "I have a business opportunity, but I can't tell you until we get to the meeting. "

Ted Turner came over and talked to us about investing $10,000. He said he had some land in Issaquah. He talked to Fred and me and some of the other big honchos. I didn't make any money, but I had the honcho image.

Ted Turner was running the meeting. Back then, Issaquah was nothing but deer and bears. Now it is shopping centers and houses everywhere. Turner was buying up a lot of land out there, and he was asking for a $10,000 investment to start cable TV. I think he was just trying to get it off the ground. And we thought he was just Amway. We thought there was no way in the world people would actually pay extra money just to watch television. So, like dummies, we turned him down. Everybody I know kept their money.

Five or six years later, I see CNN. And I think, $10,000 would be worth about $7 million right now.

I could have been home free, baby. I could have been living in "Slickwattsland."

MICHAEL JACKSON

The Westin Hotel in Seattle used to be called the Olympic Hotel. They did a commercial when I was in town that said, "Guess who had a slick time at the Olympic Hotel?"

The manager at the Olympic Hotel transferred to the Hyatt Regency in New Orleans, and so when I was traded to New Orleans in 1978, the manager gave me the top floor at the Hyatt Regency, which at the time was the swankiest hotel in town—it still is one of the best hotels there. My guy gave me the superstar suite.

If anyone big came to town—Michael Jackson, Lola Falana, whomever—when anyone came to town to perform or whatever, they couldn't get that room.

That was my room for six months for $15 a day. You talk about having a little Wilt Chamberlain in me then—I had all my suits and about 20 pairs of shoes. Oh man, I thought I was "Baby Wilt."

Everybody kept wondering how I had the room—all the players, everybody. Oh, I made some enemies. I had enemies as soon as I got off the plane there. Like I said, I was a victim of my own success, because people don't want to hear how good you have it. When they find out, they want to bring you down.

Anyway, in 1978, Michael Jackson came to town with all of his brothers, but they couldn't get my room. When they found out who was staying there, I received one of the best compliments I've ever heard.

The older brother, he told me, "Whenever we all get together to play basketball, we all fight about who is going to be Slick Watts."

In a way, though, it was so strange. I used to sit home and watch the Jackson Five when I was a kid. We are almost the same age—maybe five years apart—but to me, Michael is older than I am because he was on television when he was six years old. When he was six, I was 11 or 12, but he was my hero.

When I met him, he was talking all nice and light. He had that same little voice, but he was dark-skinned then.

MUHAMMAD ALI

I met Muhammad Ali in Chicago. We were playing the Bulls. He came to the game with his sister, wife, and daughter. They said they were Slick fans, and they wanted to meet me. When they came back to the locker room, I met Ali.

Then we were staying at the Hyatt Regency in Kansas City—the same hotel where the floating walkways collapsed in 1981 and killed a hundred people—and we were in the lobby, and Ali came up to us and started playing with us. Tommy Burleson and he were shadow boxing, and he told Tommy he could knock him out. Afterwards, we went to the bar and hung out, shot the bull.

Then, in 1978, when Ali fought Leon Spinks, I was playing for the Jazz. I had met President Carter here in Seattle in 1976. President Carter's mother was at the same hotel, headed to the fight. I was coming out of the Hyatt Regency in New Orleans, and standing next to me was Ms. Carter.

We got to talking, and the Secret Service approached and said, "Come on, you guys, let's go."

They picked me right up, took me with them, and sat me down at the fight next to Ms. Carter.

Pistol Pete later asked me, "How in the hell did you get down there?"

Seattle was my town when I was there, but New Orleans was Pistol's town. Pistol and the boys were about 18 or 20 rows back. Man, he was pissed that I got that close. I was so close that the blood from the punches got on my suit.

After the fight, they shipped us back out and took us back to the hotel. When we got back, Larry Holmes was in the lobby. That was a big night.

A STAR OF STARS

The same thing that happened at that Ali fight—getting shuffled along out of pure luck—happened to me at the All-Star game in Miami, too.

In 1990, Schick shaving cream did a commercial with Magic Johnson and me. I was Slick with my head, and he was slick with his play. They put me on a box in the ad, and I look like I am six foot nine, too. We had to shave about 50 times before we got the right take.

When I met Magic, he had the softest hands. Softest hands I ever felt in my life. I figured that was why he was such a good passer and shooter.

Anyway, the ad was supposed to be in just two magazines, but it did so well that it was placed in about 75 magazines. It was one of the ads of the year.

I got paid $5,000 for it. Magic got $100,000. They tried to keep it quiet, but every airport I went in, there we were, in all the magazines. So, my lawyer wrote them back, and I ended up getting $20,000 more.

Schick had sent me to Miami as their representative. We had to sign autographs together. As part of the deal, Schick said they would get us tickets to the All-Star game.

When I got to the game, I saw about 12 black crows sitting there, right over my shoulder. We were two feet from the top wall, it was so high. The NBA had placed all the players up there. And I was like, "Where is the respect for the players?"

So I walked downstairs, and while I was walking around, a guy I knew from New Orleans saw me and said, "Slick Watts, how you doing? Come sit here with me."

I was kicking back. I didn't pay a penny, and I was in the front row, enjoying the game.

All the other players were asking: "How in the hell did you get down there?"

I remember teasing Xavier McDaniel about it, because he was making $5 million a year, and I was the one sitting in the front row.

DUCK

I used to play doubles tennis with Rick Barry. We often played mixed doubles. I felt I was quicker and better than Rick. With my quickness, I always felt that a man six foot six couldn't beat me on the tennis court. I know Rick, though—I'm sure he felt he was better.

Rick had a big serve. There were rumors that he had served against some of the pros and aced them. I didn't seem to have that much trouble returning it, but he was notorious for his serve.

Rick was a very dominating competitor, and he didn't let up when he served against the ladies. I didn't have the killer instinct to serve hard against whoever his partner was, but Rick, he was good at popping you hard.

He used to say, "If you got me out on the court, you better be ready to play."

Rick has a different personality. That's why I never wanted to consider myself a superstar, because it comes with a powerful, powerful ego. Nobody ever measures up to a superstar. Most superstars are me, myself, and I—and no one else. That's why they take 30 shots a game.

ROCK N' ROLL

There was a band from Bellingham, Washington—just south of the Canadian border—that named itself after me. I didn't even know it until I had people tell me, "You were in Bellingham last week, I know you were."

I didn't know what all these people were talking about. I'd get calls and people would ask me why I didn't call them if I was in town that week. But after I retired, I had a cleaning business called Slick and Clean. We had the contract to clean all the Bank of Americas in Washington. I was in a bank one day in Mount Vernon, and I saw a poster of this band that had my name. Then I knew why all these people were calling me.

The crazy part is, they used my name—but I guess it is not my name. Apparently, you have to patent "Slick." I didn't patent it.

Pat Riley patented *Threepeat*, which I can't believe. You mean to tell me he patented *Threepeat*, and he makes money whenever somebody uses it on a T-shirt?

But I didn't patent "Slick Watts." I never even thought about it. I was just rolling with the punches. I never took myself that seriously. Right now, somebody has my web addresses, and I can't get it. Slick Watts, Watts Slick, and Slick13Watts. They are doing their thing, getting their hits. I can't do anything about it. I hope they are having fun. I hope they are not doing anything too crazy with my name.

With the band, I look at it as a compliment. I wish they were as big as Pearl Jam. Then I would be trying to collect some money.

CHAPTER 8

SONICS PERSONALITIES

SPENCER HAYWOOD

I called Spencer "The Captain." He was a leader on our team. He was a big guy who wore his emotions on his sleeve—above all, Spencer wanted to be respected.

He came from a small town in Mississippi. He didn't go through championships like Bill Russell, but he went through some of the same things that boost a man's ego—the Olympics, tearing down rims, strutting out of high school with the NBA and ABA fighting over him.

Spencer once said to me (and others) that he was responsible for every one of these young black millionaires. He may be right. But I guess people hate it when that individual says it himself— better for somebody else to say it, and I think that hurts Spencer, because he likes to say it sometimes. I'm not alone in thinking that he should let other people make that statement.

As a player who played this game, he deserves to have his number retired in Seattle. He created much excitement for the city of Seattle. He might say things that some people don't like to hear him say, but—from a fan's viewpoint—his number deserves to be retired.

He embodied the word excitement for this city. He was a bell-ringer—saying his name was like saying the word Christmas.

SONICS OWNER SAM SCHULMAN

Sam was an interesting owner—God rest his soul. Sam was cool. He had a little player in him. He would get on the plane with us and try to talk with the players, with the brother-like wave in his voice. He would give you high fives. I loved Sam and the way he mingled with his guys.

However, he could be tight with that pocket. He would let that pocket go every once in a while. His signings of Spencer and Brisker opened up big money to other owners. Back in those days, there was no other franchise here, so he did a good job of letting the community know the Sonics were their team.

I loved Sam, but he didn't pay me—I should be upset with him. But who knows? Back then, people who got money got into drugs and things. Look at Spencer and David Thompson and Micheal Ray Richardson. So who knows? Not getting that money may have saved my life.

FRED BROWN

Fred Brown was one of my favorite teammates. We had the chance to meet in college. Well, not so much meet. I met him, in a sense, but he didn't meet me.

I was a fan, excited about meeting players. Fred was going to a junior college in Waterloo, Iowa, and I was going to a junior college in Des Moines called Grand View Junior College. When

Fred transferred to the University of Iowa, I used to go there to watch him play.

Normally, I couldn't get in because the place was always full, and I didn't have any money anyway. I had a little hole in the side of the gym, and I used to watch the game through the little hole. Me and my boys would take turns looking though the hole.

Fred and John Johnson were playing then. Fred was dancing. Just dancing. Girls were going crazy. My eyes were big and round, like saucers. And they had J.J. and Fred. They were rolling. That place was rocking.

J.J. would bring it up the court, and Fred would go to the corner. J.J. would find Fred, and Fred would score. They were rocking. They didn't know who I was, and I didn't really know who they were, but I knew they were big-time in the state of Iowa.

I would go back to my gym and practice and try to be Fred Brown. After watching a game like that, all the people would get you hyped. You could go in the gym and shoot all night.

When I came up here to Seattle, I met Fred. I knew him, but he didn't know me. He calls me Junior—Russ is Daddy, and I'm Junior. When I tell him that story about Iowa, he says, "Shut up, Junior."

FINDING FRED

I call Fred one of my favorite teammates because he understood that when I went to the middle, he knew how to get open. And I could find him. Oh, I could find him.

I dished to him because I had confidence in him. I was surprised when he missed open shots. When I hit the lane, his man was forced to give me a layup or leave Fred open.

Fred wouldn't miss. If he missed, I was coming right back to him because I knew he would not miss twice. Tom Burleson would have a dunk or Fred would have the 30-footer. Guess where I would go? I'm serious. Fred would hit it. He knew how to catch it, and he knew how to flip it.

JACK SIKMA

Jack was one of my favorite big men. Jack was a guy who didn't have jumping ability or so-called "great talent." He was a lot like Dave Cowens. He would work and put the body on you. He was a great passer who understood the game.

He scared the hell out of me in practice because I used to come in for a lay-up and he wouldn't go for the ball. He would just go for the body. I'll tell you something: there was a quiet message he was sending to me.

"Don't come in here."

Most guys will block your shot and will talk, but Jack would turn into your body, and it would hurt. He would knock the crap out of you and not even look at you. That does more to your psyche than anything. He just acted like he didn't hit you, and that told you that he was going to hit you again because he didn't even think he hit you yet.

So I would turn the corner on Jack in practice, I would go wide and head the other way.

DENNIS JOHNSON

Dennis began to change a little bit after he got the MVP of the Finals in 1979. I wasn't playing for the Sonics anymore, but I still used to play with these guys in the summers over on Mercer Island.

We used to be two guys who could bump and grind and fight out there on the court. After he got the MVP, he was like, "Don't touch me. Don't touch me. Don't foul me. Let me make a layup."

He changed. As I said, you can be a victim of your own success. Now he is back to his old self—real nice guy again.

BOB HOPKINS

Hopkins still lives over on Mercer Island. He still loves the game. I thought, and I still think, he has one of the smartest basketball minds in the world. I just think he wasn't prepared for the professional ego. He was too intense for NBA players.

He believed basketball should be played with a passion, and that passion starts with defense. He thought that you should cut your opponent off at the baseline. He felt that, if you are six foot ten and can dunk a ball backwards, you should be able to get your hand up defensively. Bob was like, "You can put your hands down, let a guy get 44 on you and not get in a fight! There is no blood?"

He had a passion for the game. I think his passion was too great for the athletes. I thought he was responsible for getting the players who won the championship. But he will never get credit for it.

They should put a little picture of Bob by Lenny's picture in the Hall of Fame. As far as basketball minds go, there is no greater basketball mind than Bob Hopkins.

ZOLLIE VOLCHOK

Zollie was the team's general manager, and I loved him. Zollie was much like Lenny Wilkens. He is the kind of guy that when you grow up, you want to be like. He was smooth. He knows when to give a little and when to take a little. He was a real smoothie. He still says to me, "I must admit, we never did pay you. And I feel badly about that."

MIKE GREEN

Mike Green was as skinny as a pole—skinniest center to ever play the game. He looked like he weighed about 185 pounds—seven feet, about 185. You could bump him, and he would fly everywhere. But he could block shots.

He used to drink that ginseng before the games to get himself all wired. Ginseng filled his locker. He was a piece of work. He knew a ton of people. Every city we went into—Mike knew everybody.

DEAN TOLSON

Dean Tolson was the only guy who was cut about 15 times. They cut him, and he always came back. Russell would cut him one week, he would come back and play. Then he'd cut him another week, he'd come back and play.

He got cut about 15 times and never got his three years in. He got ready to get his pension, and they said he was two months short. He called me and said, "Slicky Slick"—because he calls me Slicky Slick—"I went to get my pension and they told me I was two months short. You got your pension yet?" He was hurting. He didn't make his pension—two months short because Russell cut him so many times.

KENNEDY McINTOSH

Kennedy was a deep guy. He came from the Chicago Bulls, supposed to be a good player, and he couldn't be intimidated. He was an intimidator. You couldn't get to him. They said he was out in left field.

Kennedy was something else. He would say some things—he was deeper than Russ—that left you out there. You were left trying to find the punch line or the meaning that could help your life, or try to make sense of what he said. You would just shake your head and say, "What the hell did he say?" He was deep.

Russell would get in the huddle, and McIntosh would look at Russell right in the eye. Russell would say, "Why is that m-----f----r looking at me like that for, Slick?" He was deeper than Russ was. I mean, Russ would call time out and say something, and Kennedy would just stare. Russ ended up letting him go quick.

JOHN HUMMER

John was a philosopher. He would define the play. He was kind of like Bill Walton—but he had bad feet. He ran like he was in wet cement. You heard him when he ran up and down the floor. He was like Herman Munster.

He was smart. He was from Princeton, and he was a Princeton guy on the court, too. He would stop and say, "You guys, you need to go to the back door, and then you need to come around, and then you need to set a pick."

We were like, "Shut up." Ol' John, boy, he could break a play down.

He would get on the plane and give me advice. "Slick, this is what you need to do with your money—this is what you need to invest in."

I'd say: "Yeah, $15,000. With $15,000, I'm going to invest in an apartment and a car."

WALT HAZZARD

I always had a ton of respect for Walt. After I took the first one or two balls from him in practice, I was afraid. When I saw him in the dressing room, I tried to keep it short and stay out of his way. He wasn't a politician, but he was older than I was, and I used to see him at UCLA. Walt Hazzard and John Wooden—he was part of that storybook stature. To actually play against him in practice every day was an honor.

Around that time, the Muslims were slowly beginning to show their heads. They were on the street corners, and in the Central Area they would stand around passing out pamphlets. Next thing I knew, Walt Hazzard was involved in it.

I had trouble saying his new name, Madhi Abdul-Rahman, so I continued to call him Walt. He would say, "My name is not Walt Hazzard. What did I tell you my name was?"

So we started calling him Rahman.

I was impressed because he said to me one day he knew it was time for him to retire when he started making a move on me, and when he would lean one way I would be in front of him taking the ball. I was proud because he was an All-Star and a great player, but I also felt bad about it because he was one of my heroes.

He had a stroke recently. My guess is it was because he used to smoke a ton of cigarettes. I couldn't believe how many cigarettes he used to smoke between games and practices and at halftime. He used to smoke in the locker room.

Some say that Wilt Chamberlain used to eat a pie at halftime. I never saw Wilt eat pie, but that was the rumor, Wilt would eat a lemon pie. Whatever—it didn't affect Wilt much . . . or maybe it did. Walt had a stroke, and Wilt up and died.

TOM BURLESON

As a teammate, Tommy Burleson was one of the warmest, kindest big men I ever met. He was my roommate on the road. I loved him to death. He had decent hands, so I didn't mind playing with him because he would catch it and dunk it.

He loved playing with me. When I made a good play, he would kiss me right on top of my head. I would say, "I'm not going to give you the ball any more because you kiss me on top of the head." He would still do it. Kiss me right on the court. He was very emotional. You had to love that, though. I made a good pass to him, and he would just lay a big wet kiss on top of my bald head.

I had to laugh. I told my wife, "He is always kissing me on my head every time I make a good pass." Since all I did was pass, I received many kisses. It's always good to see him. When I do, he is still emotional, and he still kisses me, just as if we were still kids on the court.

LEONARD GRAY

He is another guy that I call a silent intimidator. The Big Fella and Leonard had some battles. They used to have some staring battles, just looking at each other. Who was the strongest? Who had the strongest personalities? Who had the strongest stare?

One of the guys Russell brought in as a small forward, Leonard was thick—about 270. He could set a pick and had the softest jump shot in the world for a guy six foot eight and over.

For a guy under six foot three, Fred had the softest jump shot. But for a big guy, Leonard did. He shot it around that free throw line. He could set a pick and pop out much better than Karl Malone. I used to love to run the pick and roll with the slide out with him. I used to love to go to his side because he could wipe a poor boy's head off. He could put a guard on his hip, then get the ball and shoot it.

His career changed when he and Russell had a squat, and Russell sent him to Washington, D.C. He would have been paid because he could dance. We used to call him the "Big Dancing

Bear." Man, he could dance. He was soft on his feet—soft as a big bear.

With Russ, if you did not give ground to him, something had to give, or someone had to go. Russ was the victim of the young up-and-coming athlete—they call it hip-hop now, but I call it the young, advanced athletes beginning to change. Leonard was the start of the new-school kid. He was big, fast, he could dunk, could move like a guard—not like the big guys Russ played against.

I thought Leonard was the first of the big young forwards who could play. Leonard could ball.

PAUL SILAS

Paul was much like Lenny Wilkens—a politician, but he would light you up, really put the wood on you. He was probably the inventor of the wood. He would make sure to put a body on you. Man, he would do that well.

We used to call him "35." That was his number. We used to say, "Hey, 35, you going to lunch? You going with us?" He was a great rebounder. I thought he and Wayne Embry were the two best on-the-floor rebounders in the history of the game. When I say on-the-floor rebounder, I mean wait until the ball comes down, and grab it. He did a good job of grabbing it, too. When he got it, it belonged to him.

I think he helped Jack Sikma a lot by showing him all of that. Paul taught Jack how to put the wood on people—he taught Jack how to knock the crap out of someone, but be nice to them.

That's why I said Paul is a nice little politician. He is an old-school guy. He knew how to hang around and get in the right doors, and that is why he is coaching today.

ROD DERLINE

Rod had no issues. Just came in and shot it. You couldn't hit him in the mouth and feel good about it, so you just played him hard and left it all to basketball. No trash talking. He was just smooooooth. He didn't have any baggage. A great guy to play with, a great guy to know.

JOBY WRIGHT

Joby Wright was a mean guy until Brisker broke his jaw. That punch discounted all the hype he created for himself. It messed up his whole career. He finally found out he wasn't the big dog he thought he was.

FRANK FURTADO

Frank Furtado should do a book on his own life—I bet he has some incredible stories. He was the best trainer. You could go get him out of bed, and he would rub you and massage you. He wasn't like most trainers who said, "Get your ass over to the table and ice yourself."

Frank was a great trainer.

JACK CURRAN

Jack Curran was our trainer at first. He later went to the Lakers. When I saw Jack, he went big-time on me because he was with the Lakers, and he had Kareem and Jerry West. I saw Jack, and I said, "You the man, Jack."

Unlike Frank Furtado, Jack didn't play any rubbing down.
Jack would say, "If your back aches, you got to do it yourself."
Jack would tape your ankle, but he didn't play no touching.

CHAPTER 9

LEAGUE PERSONALITIES

PAT RILEY

When Pat played against us, he was a little ol' guy sitting on the bench with long hair and didn't play much. Then he got Magic Johnson, and he came out of the booth and won some championships. His hair is all rolled back, and his image has changed—you see him somewhere, and he won't even say hello. Fame does strange things to people. That's why I'm glad when I got mine—and mine was quick—but what it made me do was appreciate it. Overall, I would say Pat was a solid player, but I would say he was a better coach.

CALVIN MURPHY

"They used to trip each other all game," a former teammate said of me and Calvin Murphy. "They used to hate each other."

Maybe this is why.

I played with Calvin Murphy, and I played against Murphy. The only way I could get to Murphy, though, was to talk about his mama. Boy, he didn't like you to talk about his mama.

One night, he dropped around 38 on me. "You can't stop me m-----f----r, you can't stop me. You can't stop me." He wouldn't stop talking.

So I said, "Calvin, me and your mama was rolling last night."

We played them two weeks later, and he had around four points. He didn't want to shoot; he just wanted to fight. "I'm going to kick your ass. I'm going to get ya."

So every time I saw him before we would play, I would say: "Calvin, me and your mama."

It was dirty. I shouldn't have done that, but he could shoot. I pulled a Bill Russell on him, though—I found a way to get in his head.

I didn't even know his mama.

When I was traded to Houston, Murphy would say, "You got to come party with me. I had a party New Year's Eve. And all the women are still in the house."

When he told me that, it was June. I laughed—I have to admit, that was a good one.

BILL WALTON

Bill is one of my all-time favorite big men—just because of how he played the game. I remember going down to Los Angeles during one offseason, and when he knew I was in town, he called me, and we all went over to UCLA.

I was so impressed how Bill got all us together, all of us so-called NBA stars: Dave Bing, Archie Clark, Nate Archibald, Marques Johnson, Lucius Allen, Gail Goodrich, and some UCLA guys were there.

Bill actually held a complete practice. He was a player, and he actually organized a complete practice with all those egos in the gym. We'd then play a pickup game. Bill was walking through stuff. I was amazed how he got all of us to do it, and he was in control of it. John Wooden had gotten into his blood. Bill is a piece of work. After that, I always thought he would be a good coach.

BUT NOT FUN TO TRAVEL WITH . . .

Back in those days, Bill was a trip. Back then, we would play each other, and then the next day both teams would sometimes get on the same plane.

On this particular flight, Bill was in first class. It's hard to imagine now, because he is such a politically correct guy—but his junk was out. The stewardess just started looking around, not knowing what to say. He was dead asleep. He had his foot up on the bulkhead and his privates were just hanging out because his shorts were too short.

Bill came a long way. That is something I will never forget—getting on the plane and seeing him sitting there in a pair of shorts that were too short. It reminded me of a lady on a corner with a dress that was coming up and was too short.

Still, Bill was one of the most intelligent players I ever played against.

KAREEM ABDUL-JABBAR

After I discovered that Kareem didn't like direct contact, Kareem found out that I was a good little player—so he started elbowing me. One day, I came by a pick, and he caught me in the ribs. The entire side of my body just shut down completely. I couldn't fight this big old guy. I dreamed about that elbow.

So I grew my fingernails. I grew 'em. I grew 'em long. The next time we played, I came by a pick, and I took his neck, and boy . . . I scratched him good.

After the game, he gave me five. I thought he was going to come over to kick my butt, but instead he said, "Good game, Watts."

I got his respect. I will never forget that. That was one of my awakenings. He never hit me again like that.

MOSES MALONE

I played with Mo in Houston, and he was a great rebounder. People say you can't be selfish when you are an assist player, but that is a lie. Sometimes you can hold the ball too long or sometimes you can pass and get assists. I used to love assists, so my way of being selfish was by passing.

I would come in and have a lay-up, but I wanted that dime. So I would give it back to Mo instead of shooting the lay-up. He was always telling me to shoot the damn thing. He wanted me to miss so he would get a rebound. He wanted rebounds. I wanted assists. When it came to scoring, he wanted to score off a missed opportunity. He didn't want to score off an assist.

Calvin Murphy, boy, you didn't have to tell him to shoot. He, Rudy T, and Mike Newlin—they used to love me. They used to tell me after practice, "You are the best guard we got." They used to try to fill up my head because they knew I would get them the ball.

With Mo, they used to say that he would miss five or six shots on purpose and get five or six rebounds. Moses actually used to miss those shots point-blank. He wouldn't dunk it; he would just keep throwing it up there. We used to tease him about it. We'd say: "Mo, you try to pad your rebounds. There is no way you should have missed that shot."

But he did have little hands. His hands were no bigger than mine were; so that might have been a reason that it took him so long to put those shots in.

JOHN HAVLICEK

John Havlicek is someone I looked up to and respected because Bill Russell respected him so much. When we came to Boston, John was the focus of every game discussion.

He was always a professional. He moved without the ball. He did a lot of stuff in the community. He was a guy I looked up to, and it was a privilege to play against him. He didn't have any issues like most other guys—he just played the game. You couldn't get him into any trash talking. You'd bump into each other, he'd ask you if you were all right. He was always a very respectful guy.

DAVE COWENS

Dave Cowens and I were wild when it came to hustle. We would hit the ground a lot. I remember in Boston one night, we both went for a loose ball. He was sliding. I was sliding. That's the kind of players we were.

One night, I shot a bad shot. He came to me during the game and said, "I've never seen you shoot a shot that bad." He wasn't making fun of me. He knew that I was one of those role players who worked hard and did everything fundamentally sound. After I had taken one of those wild fade-aways, he asked me, "Are you all right?"

I was freaked out that he had any respect for my game and knew that I usually made good decisions as a point guard.

TOM HEINSOHN

I used to have Tom Heinsohn talk about me all the time when he coached because I used to disrupt their offense. I used to gamble. He would say, "All he does is gamble and play zone."

I knew that Russell and Tom Heinsohn had all the same plays because of that "Boston Concept." So I just played like I played in practice. I just played the passing lanes because I knew they were going to run all the same stuff, like all those Boston boys do, running all Red Auerbach's plays.

PISTOL PETE MARAVICH

We played together for about 35 games. I got out of Pete's way. Pete was the man in New Orleans.

We went on a winning streak—and then he got hurt. He broke his knee. Randy Smith had us on a fast break, and Pete jumped up on the air, hooked the ball behind his leg, landed, and broke his kneecap.

RICK BARRY

I played with Rick for a season in Houston. Rick was much like Russell in a way—both proud men, very self-assured and outspoken. They always think what they have to say is more important than what you have to say. So you get out of the way and listen. If you catered to Rick, he could be a great guy—as long as you didn't rock his boat. I didn't rock the boat.

I hung with him a few times at Studio 54 in New York. Sometimes he would call and ask me to hit the town with him. Even though he was Rick Barry on the court, in my heyday, I was Slick Watts on the court and *off* the court because of my symbol—the bald head—and that opened some swanky doors. Many guys more big-time than me—like Rick—would stand in many lines. Some of them didn't have much to distinguish themselves.

Out of uniform, they just stood there looking like tall bankers or lawyers.

When I would go in there and take my hat off, I'd get in.

I would say, "Slick Watts, I got Rick Barry with me."

And they'd say, "You got Rick Barry with you?"

And they'd get all excited—at first it was just a bunch of tall animals in line at the door.

I was always a good public relations guy.

RATING RICK

I thought Rick was probably the first or second best forward to ever play the game. He would come off the pick, shoot that old ugly scoop shot. He'd get you up in the air and shoot that two-handed scoop. He could dominate the ball—probably one of the best guys to play with as a point guard.

He and John Johnson probably developed the position *point forward*. They were players who could see the floor, get the ball to people, as well as score. I thought Rick was right up there with the top small forwards.

You also have to go to Larry Bird. Larry worked his way into the best ever. He probably doesn't want to hear this, but he was slow when he came into the league. Yet, he taught himself how to master the NBA. He taught himself how to get good.

I thought he and Rick were the top two forwards I've ever seen. As for centers—you have to go with the brothers: Russ, Wilt, Kareem, and Shaq.

Point guards—you probably have to go with the brothers.

But that small forward position, I thought the white boys ate that up.

JULIUS ERVING

Dr. J probably doesn't want me to say that about Rick and Larry being the best, but I thought Dr. J was the most exciting to play against. He started all that Mike stuff. Playing against him was a treat. I'd call home and say, "Mama, I played against Dr. J."

One night, I scored a bunch on him. He came at me to block my shot and I shot that little scoop shot I had over him. I didn't care then about anything else. Win or lose, all I cared about was I got a scoop over the Doctor.

It was something to tell your grandkids about.

WALT FRAZIER

I liked Walt because he was clean, and he taught me how to be the Great Gatsby. That's what Wally Walker calls me now. When I played with Wally, I had this big ol' fur coat, and I would pull the hood over my head, so Wally started calling me Gatsby. However, I really learned that from Walt, because I was trying to be clean just like Clyde.

He was Clyde Frazier. He had the big ol' hat on. I had on the high shoes and the one-piece outfits unzipped to my belly button. I look at that stuff now—we were so stupid, but we thought we were cool. We used to go to Studio 54 and those nightclubs around the Garden. I'd walk in there with Walt.

Boy, a small-town boy hanging out with Walt Frazier at Studio 54? That was something else.

DR. WALT

Walt inspired me to play well—he was smooth.

Walt would tell me, "You can steal balls like I can. But one problem you got, you try to steal them all the time. Now you watch me. What you need to try to do, you need to time your stealing, wait until it means something."

That was a good point. He would fake at the ball 12 times all night, but he would wait until it was 88-86, and then he would go get it. He would set you up all night, and you would say to yourself, "He's been doing this all night."

Then when it was 88-86 and you need a big basket—boom—he'd get a steal, and we'd lose by four.

He'd say: "You are good, but you use too much of your energy. Wait until the last four minutes of the game."

EARL MONROE

Earl was much like I was. He went to a small school—Winston-Salem—and I went to Xavier. So I had a lot of respect for Earl—he is another guy I liked to emulate as a player.

He was nice to talk to, but he was your enemy on the court. He would get you down in the post, and he could be rocking you back and forth—and you'd start rocking back and forth with him—and then he'd stop and shoot right over the top of your nose.

You'd say to yourself, "Now why the hell didn't I block that?" He'd just stop and look at you.

He would do it every time, and he would never jump. He'd shoot it from around his chest—right in your face. And you would scream at yourself, "WHY CAN'T I BLOCK THIS?"

It took me years to understand that when Earl got to rocking, don't rock with him—just stand there.

GAIL GOODRICH

Gail was very sneaky. I was having a good rookie year, and we were going down to Los Angeles to play the Lakers. I had blood in my eyes—I wanted to kick his tail real bad. I really wanted to play well that night because he would come off those picks with Jerry West, and they were balling. I was getting ready to play Jerry and Gail. I was pumped. I was going to wear his little butt out.

Russ was getting me ready, getting in my head: "Gail's going to kick your butt tonight, Slick." I had my game face on. I was like a boxer. My fingernails were long. I was ready.

Then, just before tip-off, Gail came up to me and said, "Slick, you are having a great year. You are a great player. You are going to be an all-pro."

It just let the air out of me. I was like: "Oh Gail, just kiss me tonight, baby. Oh Gail, you make me feel so good."

He seduced me with that, and he went off on me that night. He wore me out. Went around picks, shot that little soft jumper, killed me with that little left hand.

Russ later asked me: "He tricked you, didn't he?"

I said, "Yup, he pulled the old veteran trip on me."

That was a good one on me, though. I'll never forget that. That was an old Boston, Bill Russell trick. I got so mad that I whooped his tail the next time I was in town.

He tried to come up and talk to me before the game again, but I told him not to talk to me.

NORM VAN LIER

Norm was another sneaky guy. Playing against him was a little like playing against myself, but I was quicker and could handle the ball better. He had made all-pro defense. I got ready to make the All-Star team, but he beat me out by something like 1,000 votes. I led him the entire year in votes, but Chicago people just plugged the box, and he beat me out the last day.

Chicago is bigger than Seattle—what are you going to do?

JERRY SLOAN

Jerry Sloan would fight a lot. John Brisker and Jerry Sloan, I would have paid $10,000 to see those two fight each other. Neither ever backed down. When we got into confrontations, those are the two you got behind—John Brisker and Jerry Sloan.

RANDY SMITH

Randy Smith was a trip. He was one of my greatest opponents. I thought I was fast, but he was actually a roadrunner. He would just blow by you. I remember going by him for a lay-up, and normally when that happened I didn't have to worry about the guy any more, but I always knew Randy was back there. He was the fastest human being. When Bob Hayes and all those guys were doing the 100, I thought Randy Smith could have beat him. I have never seen a human being that fast. And he's still in shape, too.

CHARLEY SCOTT

Charley Scott was one of the better guards at the time, though he had a Rick Barry attitude. Charley was six foot six, six foot seven, real skinny, and moved real fast. He was the fastest tall guy that I ever played against. He was almost Randy Smith-fast. He liked to take a ton of shots, and he was very competitive. He was a tough player to defend.

NATE "TINY" ARCHIBALD

Nate was very quiet—didn't talk no trash. He just tried to bring it to you. The only chance you had to play against him was to get him back on the defensive end because offensively he worked you so hard. He had led the league in scoring and assists. I had some real decent games against Nate, but he had that left hand. A little man who leads the league in scoring and assists—he writes history. That was quite an achievement for him—something he can carry to his grave.

SAM LACEY

Sam Lacey is another of those guys who would ring your bell. He would do it differently than Jack Sikma, though. Jack would hit you and walk away. Sam would ring your bell and then sing in your ear about it. He'd say, "Don't bring your little bald-headed ass in here no more." He would cuss you and give you that look. Sam scared me.

Sam was the one who really made you think he was mad. You actually thought he would hurt you. He had that I-am-mad-at-the-world look. He was ready to rebel on you.

CLIFFORD RAY

Everyone called him "Yo." I would go to his house during the winter, and in November or December, he'd have a Christmas tree up.

Then we'd go to a golf tournament, and I'd go down there to Oakland during the summer, and that Christmas tree would still be up.

He'd say, "It is Christmas every day in my life."

So he had me doing that. My wife would get pissed at me and be like, "Take that Christmas tree down." And I'd say, "I want to be like 'Yo.' I don't want to take my Christmas tree down. I want it to be Christmas every day."

WORLD B. FREE

I played against Lloyd B. in college in a tournament in Kansas City. To get a chance to meet him in the pros was very surprising. In college, he played the same way. Shot the ball a lot. Shot the ball high—looked like it took two minutes for the ball to go through the goal.

Lloyd taught you a ton of things. If you got up close, he would kick you. Actually kick you—kind of like Karl Malone. His legs would go up high, and he would kick you right in the groin.

Guess who would be at the free throw line?

So just before he shot, I used to run at him, and then circle him and get out of the way. Because if you stayed in the way, he would kick you, nothing but net, and get a three-point play.

Of the guys I played against, he was the most difficult guy to defend because he could go right, left, up and down.

OSCAR ROBERTSON

By the time I got a chance to play against the Big O, he had slowed a little bit. He still had the real strong ego—he didn't like you to touch him, and he didn't like you to hack him. He'd look at me like, "Are you crazy? I'm the Big O." But I was little. I couldn't play tall. If you brought the ball down, I would scratch you anywhere but in your jock.

His last two years, I got a chance to play against him when he was with Milwaukee—he and Kareem together. To him, I probably wasn't even on the floor. To him, my eyes were this big, because it was the Big O. He knows how to put you on that hip and elbow you. I bet I had four fouls in the first two minutes playing him.

JERRY WEST

Jerry played with Gail Goodrich, and sometimes I would try to use my speed to force West to the left.

He would still go right, and Russ would say, "Slick, did you watch the video? Did you watch the tape at home? That man likes to go right."

And I'd say, "Coach, I used to watch him play you, and he would go right and get 40, too."

Russ would look at me like I was crazy and say, "Get the f--- out of here."

CHAPTER 10

1976-77

The 1976-77 season is best known as Bill Russell's final season as coach of the Sonics—perhaps his biggest failure in professional basketball.

After two straight seasons of making the playoffs, we missed the postseason. Big Bill had become too much of a soap opera. He had beat down too many people. He had sent away too many talented players. He couldn't get along with anyone, and rumors were starting to circulate about his work habits. He was being booed by the home fans—it was just time for him to go.

I have to admit, though—I never thought I'd see it. I never thought Russ would be fired. I thought Sam Schulman had given him everything, and he was going to let Big Russ decide when he wanted to leave. Of course, Russell will tell you—to this day—that it was his choice to leave, but I know better.

SETTING THE RECORD STRAIGHT

Russ says in his book that he did not even want to coach the season because he had been turned off the previous year. He cites the facts that we made the playoffs, lost to Phoenix in the first round, and then we would not give any of the playoff money to various people.

"They withheld even the complimentary amounts customarily given to such support people in the franchise as the trainer, people in the front office, and the assistant coach," Russell wrote in *Second Wind*. "I couldn't believe it. The money involved was a trifling sum compared to what they made."

That is probably true—because we were learning from him. We were learning from our leader. Get paid and get all the paper you can get, you know what I am saying? Just don't spread the wealth to anybody else. Look where all the promises he made me about making me a millionaire got me.

Yeah, we probably picked up some of his habits. You know, some guys don't ever look at themselves. "You guys should not do this. You shouldn't do that," they say.

Well, sometimes it comes from the top. The top needs to look at itself, too, but Russ didn't see it that way. He saw us as a group of kids, and he was Daddy.

That whole ride he took with Boston—it was successful, but what does it all mean other than you played on some good championship teams? What does it mean in the whole stretch of life? Does it cure cancer? If it does, then I'll be the first to bow. The fact is, it's a game, and we should keep it that way.

Russ thought we were kids, and he wanted you thinking how Daddy thought.

BURNED

The one thing about that NBA life, it can fool you. It can make you feel you are precious and handsome. You can think these women are into you—but these ladies, I call them catchers.

This one time, a friend of mine bought a girl from Seattle a plane ticket to meet him in Denver for a road trip. She didn't show up.

I was lying in bed with my wife around two or three in the morning, and my phone rang. Of course, my wife was like, "Who the hell is calling at this hour?"

I picked up the phone, and the voice said, "Slick, do you know the police in Seattle?"

"Yeah, I know the police."

"Call the police, that b---h took my money," he said.

It turned out, the woman had cashed in the first-class plane ticket that my friend bought her and used it to fly with her boyfriend to Hawaii.

The thing I laughed about most was he called me to help him get his $984 back. I couldn't do anything about it. I knew the police—but not that well.

MUSIC MAN

With my new contract, I was making twice the money as before, so I thought I had it going on. I had a little posse of a guy named Thaddeus Glade and my older brother, Dwight, who came up from Mississippi to live.

Thaddeus worked as an assistant trainer to Frank Furtado. He came up here from New Orleans. He was a trainer on my team at Xavier. He was a real big kid, and everybody loved him. He was like my right hand. I trusted him, although he and my brother did get a lot of money out of my pocket.

I had a big old black piano in the house, so the Fifth Dimension came into the house, and a guy came and played like Ray Charles.

Then my brother got the idea to start promoting shows. At the time, Teddy Pendergrass was cooking. My brother promoted shows with Teddy coming to Seattle, Portland, and Vancouver, but we had to put up $65,000 up front—which we did. He came up here, and we sold only 1,500 tickets. There weren't enough black folks living in Seattle at the time, so that cost me a lot of money. Teddy did better in Vancouver, but he still didn't sell enough tickets.

Then we tried the same thing with Marvin Gaye. Dwight tossed that on me, too. Only Marvin was worse. Marvin came up here with the Fifth Dimension, and we didn't have his orange juice mixed correctly, so he refused to sing. Can you believe it? Wouldn't sing because he didn't have the correct orange juice.

We begged him to come out. He was supposed to go on at about 9, and he came out at quarter to 11, sang until 11 o clock and said, "That's all."

I wanted to shoot my brother, but it was fun. Those were the good old days.

WHAT'S HAPPENIN'?

During the 1976-77 season, Blaine Johnson, the beat writer for the *Seattle Post-Intelligencer*, wrote a book about the team called *What's Happenin'?*

I have to say, there were some people pissed about the book, and for a while, I was one of them. Blaine was cool—he was a cat who could hang out with the players. Greg Heberlein, the beat writer for *The Seattle Times*, he was more straightforward, would come in and get his work done.

The problem was, Blaine didn't tell any of us he was writing a book. He was with us the entire season and never said a word, then out comes this tell-all. I had Blaine in my car, we were riding across the 520 bridge going to my house with my top down, and our entire conversation ended up in the book.

In fact, that's the reason that Frank Furtado would not speak with the media. He was close with Blaine, and when some of what Frank told Blaine ended up in the book, Frank stopped talking to the media for the rest of his life.

RUSSELL TAKES A HIT

This entire season was a soap opera, and because of that, Big Bill was booed at home games. Rumors started to circulate that Russ was not conducting the practices—that he was out golfing instead. The rumors weren't true—Russ was always at practice, but you know how rumors are.

Personally, I remember Russ being booed when he made some bad personnel moves, like trading Leonard Gray to Washington, but I wasn't paying much attention. I was really into that contract thing because I felt like I still wasn't making any money, and I was beginning to lead the team in minutes played, steals, assists, and community appearances. I was everywhere in the city. All you had to do was look up—I was on the buses. I was at speaking engagements. I didn't have sense enough to say no. I was crazy, really.

Then it finally started to bother me.

PUBLIC RELATIONS MESS

Toward the end of that year, I had injured my knee when I fell to the ground on a drive. It scared the hell out of me. Not so much the injury, but because I realized that my career could end at any time, I may never get the money that Russell promised me.

That injury (and a bunch of stuff before the injury) did me in. What happened was, we had gone on a long road trip—ten games. You never see those anymore, but we were gone for 19 days. I had played really well. I was finger-rolling on everybody. I led the team in scoring six of the ten games. Dr. J and Bob Lanier, all the superstars in the league, they blew up my head.

I was second in the league in assists and third in steals. I had been named All-Defensive team the year before. All the superstars started telling me how good I was, how I needed to be paid. They couldn't believe how little money I was making.

Earl Monroe told me the Sonics were dogging me. They told me how I was one of the best players in the league. In fact, there was a calendar made of NBA superstars, with all those guys—I was the superstar for December.

As I said, when I was injured, it scared me, and what was already inside of me began to spill. I felt like I should have been at least among the top six paid players on the team, and I was at the bottom.

One of the jokes on the team at the time was: "Slick, he's got everything—but a contract."

Blaine Johnson caught me in my room, and I went off.

"It's been something that has been gnawin' at me all year," I told Johnson. "I thought I could sit on it. I thought I could make it through the year and keep my mouth shut on it, but it's just been eating me up inside. I lay up here in my room, and I'm too scared to sleep, because I realize how quickly my career could end. When I got hurt in that Indiana game, I saw then that I could be through tomorrow. Kareem and Bob Lanier could stick an elbow out tomorrow and end my career like a boy squashin' a bug on a log. I play hard and do the dirty work, and for doing the dirty work I want to get compensated.

"When I hurt my knee I knew I had to do something about getting what I deserve. I been told all along that I'm a free agent and I'm lucky to be gettin' what I'm gettin'. I can't help it if people were so dumb they didn't know I could play. Now I've showed I can and I just want what I deserve. When I first came here, I had to take it, couldn't do no better, was happy to be here—now I know what I can do and they know what I can do. Let's get things to where it's fair.

"I hate to put it into words like, 'Slick Watts says pay me or trade me.' I know people think I'm making good money, and I am. But I bring people into the coliseum. I'm popular in the community—that isn't just for me, that helps the Sonics. Sam is getting compensated, Russ is getting compensated, Tommy's getting very compensated, Fred is getting compensated. There's a lot of guys getting over a hundred thousand a year, and they don't even get off the bench.

"Russ told me to be patient, and I'll get mine when I'm older. But maybe I won't be around. Maybe things will change. Maybe I'll get hurt, and I'll never get anything. I could be a nice little boy and shut up and things might be all right for everybody else. But Sam's paid millions to players who have never done a thing, and now a player who has done a lot is just asking for all that's due him."

I admit it—I said it. "Pay me or trade me." I said it on the road. When we got back, they had big headlines—not in sports, but across the A-section of the newspaper.

I think about some of this, and it seems like it was another world, or it was a book I was already reading about somebody else. I feel like it never even happened. Oh man, I thought I mattered back in those days.

It was splashed across the newspaper, and it was the talk of the town. The little ol' boy from Mississippi who was a hero was just like the rest of them. I came home and found out I was losing all my loyal fans—so I told my agent I would back off.

By then, though, the soap opera had begun. It was too late to stop it.

DECIDING RUSSELL'S FATE

Because Fred and I at the time were the team's leaders, Sam Schulman gave us a little meeting with him about Big Bill.

He asked us what we thought about Coach Russell no longer being in Seattle. I won't quote Fred, but he felt a sense of relief. We both respected Russ, but it was a sense of relief because he was the type of coach where you really had to understand him to play for him. He brought all his baggage from Boston—I am the champion, bow down to me.

Then Sam said, "All right, wait, and there will be an announcement."

Then the announcement came out that Russell was leaving.

SAVING FACE

Of course, our Daddy never would let it be known that he was fired. It is like this: Russell was such a big item, so big time, that he would never let it be thought in the community that Sam Schulman fired him.

Sam talked to Fred and me, and he had told us Russell wasn't going to be here before they announced it. We knew that Russell was going to go, but he would never let it be said he was fired.

One of Russell's issues was power. He always wanted things to be done on his terms. That's like Jim Brown. He wanted to leave on his own terms, so Jim Brown walked away from football. He and Russ thought alike. Russ wanted to make it seem like he walked away from the Sonics on his own terms.

The one thing I used to respect about Big Bill was, he always said, "For 48 minutes, you get on that floor and give me what you got. After that, I don't care what you do."

That's why I hate to hear it when today's guys say, "We played last night; I'm tired. We traveled."

Come on, you are on a plane with first class, movies, food, the whole thing. Why are you tired? That was the way I tried to pattern my game, after what Russ said: "For 48 minutes give it everything you got, because you got 23 hours and 12 minutes to rest."

Nobody else in the world has that much rest.

SWEDEN

I was coming off one of my highlight years, and the King of Sweden and Coca-Cola invited Earl Monroe, a few other NBA stars and me to do a basketball camp in Sweden. I felt privileged to demonstrate basketball in front of a king.

After we landed in Sweden, I had an experience I will never forget—playing some tennis against the great Bjorn Borg, who at the time seemed like a young boy. He was 21 years old, but he seemed young. They played on clay, and that was my first time playing on clay.

We just hit ground strokes, but you could tell he was good. He was hitting the ball well. That was a highlight for me. When I got back and saw him play John McEnroe and Jimmy Connors and all those boys, it made me feel good—another one of my highlights.

SOMETHING IS FISHY

One experience that sticks out in my mind was ordering smoked salmon in Sweden. We were having a luncheon, and I was ready for a big piece of salmon coming up—and they brought me a long piece of raw salmon.

"I ordered some smoked salmon," I told the waiter.

"Yeah, this is smoked salmon."

That was my first introduction to raw salmon. I was expecting this smoked stuff coming off the skillet or whatever, because here in America smoked salmon is cooked and smoked and preserved in a package. For $50, they brought me a raw piece of salmon.

I didn't eat it. I just let it sit there and told them to bring me something else, told them to bring me some oatmeal or something I could handle.

CHAPTER 11

DOWNFALL

BOB HOPKINS

When Big Bill left, they hired Bob Hopkins, which to me was funny because he was Russell's cousin. You would have thought that the organization wanted a clean break from Russell, given everything that happened and the way it ended—but they gave the job to Hoppy.

Right there, waiting in the wings, was Lenny Wilkens. They had hired him as general manager. They had brought him back to Seattle. He did not leave on the best terms because he wanted to be a player-coach, and Sam told him that he wanted him to be either a player or a coach—but not both. That's why Lenny was traded to Cleveland.

Everybody knew, though, that Lenny was sitting there waiting to take over. It was kind of like the situation in New York right now, where everybody knows that Isiah is sitting there waiting and eventually wants to take over.

JACK SIKMA

Jack was the other part of our little soap opera. He was from a small college—Illinois Wesleyan—and he was the Sonics' top draft pick, and nobody knew who he was or from whence he came.

Now that his number is retired and he has won a championship, everybody wants to take credit for Jack. Bob Hopkins is the one who went out and saw Jack play. Hopkins. He said: "Jack can play. He knows how to get into position. He has a step-back jumper." I remember Hopkins bragging about it, and I remember everybody saying that Hopkins was crazy.

Then Jack began to blossom. He began to show us point guards he could catch the ball. He can slide off and take that jumper. And he showed us point guards he could help on the pick-and-roll.

The pick-and-roll is a part of the game that point guards hate. Because you are going to be knocked around by some seven-footer, and your big guy is either going to let you through, or he is going to switch. Jack knew how to close out that play.

We all loved Jack. He began to flourish, and then Paul Silas took him under his wing, and he got better and better. Just don't let anybody tell you that anyone other than Bob Hopkins was responsible for Jack Sikma being in Seattle.

POOR START

Hopkins lost his job—and I probably ended up leaving Seattle—because we started the season 5-17.

Hop had the idea that Marvin Webster should be a point center. He tried to eliminate Fred and me from handling the ball almost completely. I think that is why he lost the job, but everybody has their own opinions.

Fred and I were rolling—we were playing as well as any two guys in the country at the time. Hop just came in and said that

Marvin Webster was going to be like Bill Walton. The thing about the NBA—if you win with five guys, then next year every team will have five similar guys. If you win with five new guys, next year everybody will have five similar new guys. They are copycats.

Bill Walton had won the championship in Portland, and Marvin Webster was a defender. Hop wanted him to handle the ball and have everybody cut off him. Everybody was trying to find the next Bill Walton.

Nobody could pass at the top of the key like Bill. He just knew how to do it. Marvin didn't know how to do it. It wasn't his fault. He just wasn't Bill Walton. He kept throwing it away—the ball, our season, and eventually my career in Seattle.

JAY GATSBY

In '76, Wally Walker—the Sonics' current CEO—dubbed me "Great Gatsby." I used to think I was clean. I had a jean suit with Slick embroidered on it. I had a fur coat. I was trying to be like Walt Frazier.

Walt was my hero. Every time I would go to New York or Buffalo, I would buy some threads to look like Clyde. I had black and white gangster-type shoes. I had a fur coat with a hood that I pulled up over my head. So Wally, who we had traded for in November, called me "Gatsby." In fact, he still does.

I called him "Legs." Whenever we went to a bar to have drinks, girls would say, "Who is your friend?"

"That is Wally."

They would say, "Wally, you have lovely legs."

HELLO LENNY

After they fired Hopkins, Lenny stepped in as coach, which everybody knew was going to happen.

Lenny and I had played against each other. I respect him a lot, and I always said I wanted to be like him when I grew up. Lenny is smooth. He always knows how to handle situations, whether he likes you or dislikes you. He knew how to handle the situation. He would have been a great politician.

However, Lenny didn't like my style of play. I can understand that. I was a fighter, a survivor, and a scratcher—he was smooth. So I can understand. Ice cream has to have a refrigerator. I wasn't a refrigerator—I was fire. Fire and ice don't necessarily mix.

THE FIRST SIGN

One day after Lenny took over as coach, our team went to Canlis Restaurant on Aurora Avenue—one of the nicer restaurants in town.

I had on a black velvet coat, gray slacks, black and gray shoes, gray and black tie. Guess what Lenny wore? The exact same suit. I was sitting at the head of the table. He was sitting at the other end of the table.

Sam Schulman made a statement that set me up. He said, "I wish I had 12 Slicks." What that did was make it look great to the public, and it made it look great for my image—but it created enemies. Everybody started looking at me differently, especially my teammates.

I went from the lovable, happy Slick Watts to someone who was supposed to be a superstar. As I said before, guys don't like people to be out of their place. They want to bring you down when that happens, put you back in your place.

We were sitting at this dinner, and Lenny was wearing the exact same suit that I am. Paul Silas and those guys—I love those guys, but they are so full of it—they screamed, "Who is the coach tonight?" They were kidding, but they weren't. My own teammates started to pull the plug on me.

Lenny and I wore the same suit to Canlis.
From the Donald Watts Collection

"Did y'all call each other?" they yelled. They were selling me out slowly, boy. I wasn't mad. I thought it was funny. I think about it now, and I laugh. Sitting up there, just like twins. The boys were calling me "Coach Watts." I just put my head down and smiled.

STRAW, CAMEL

The week after the dinner at Canlis, we were going on a road trip. The pilot of Northwest Airlines came over the loudspeaker when we took off and he said, "We'd like to welcome Slick Watts and the Seattle SuperSonics."

That did it. That was it. I mean—that was it, man. I didn't get off the bench that night. Do not mess with brothers who played this game and have been great. No, you stay in your place.

If I had it to do over again, I would have stayed in my place. I was a victim of my own success. I was just a country boy, and I didn't know what the hell I was doing. I was just being nice and being myself, but that was pushing me out of town. My teammates pretended they were kidding, but they were helping me get the boot, too. I will never forget that.

Little Fella—we called Lenny "Little Fella" since Russ was Big Fella—he didn't like that too much.

THE TALK

Soon after those two events happened, Lenny and I had lunch at a restaurant in Bellevue.

He sat down and told me, "Slick, this town ain't big enough for both of us."

"Coach, all I want to do is play," I said.

"I want to make some changes out there," Lenny told me.

We had won three straight with me starting after they had fired Hopkins. He said he wanted to change. I knew I couldn't play myself out of the lineup because I was still playing well. So I knew he had made up his mind.

If you are at home and your parents don't take care of you, when your step-daddy comes, you are in trouble. Lenny was my step-daddy, and Russell was my father. Then I didn't know that, but now, as I look back with maturity, I see that. Lenny wanted his people, and I wasn't one of his people.

As it turns out, not too many people could threaten Lenny's reputation. He came in with Dennis Johnson and ran Dennis out of town—after Dennis won the NBA Finals MVP. The reputation with him was he couldn't stand popular players. Dominique Wilkins, Vince Carter—everyone I talked to, they said the same thing.

My biggest thing, as a player and as a person, is my "go-getter" attitude. I wanted to play. I found that I wasn't a part of what Lenny was about—his philosophy. I was caught between my father and my step-daddy.

Little Fella had Gus Williams, Fred, and Dennis Johnson. I had played against all three of them in practice, and with them in games, so I knew that my talent stood up against all three of them.

Yet, I also knew that my so-called Daddies—Russ and Hop—had gone. I soon found out it was a "Who-loves-you-baby?" type of thing. Lenny was sitting there waiting for Hop to fall. Hop fell. Lenny was in there. After that dinner at Canlis and then that lunch, I knew I was out of there.

After that, I told Little Fella: "Coach, I don't think you have me in your plans, so send me somewhere else."

HOW TO DO IT

There was one problem with Lenny having to trade me: I was still one of the most popular figures in Seattle. Remember, this was only a year and a half after I was opening the Kingdome and named the SeaFair Grand Marshall and such. Lenny had to figure out a way to ship me out of town without taking a public relations hit. As I said, he was smooth.

First, Lenny let it be known that I wanted to be traded. He didn't mention anything about our little lunch, about him saying he wanted to make a change. He put it on me—a real smoothie. Lenny told the fans that I wanted out. I didn't want out—I just felt like I didn't want to be dropped without a decline in my abilities. Then he benched me, and he told the media that he wanted to keep me healthy in case we made a deal.

They sat me down for about a month and a half, getting little or no time. That made it worse. They wouldn't play me. In two games, I didn't even dress. I went from leading the league in steals and assists and making all-defensive team to not dressing. I was pulling a Vin Baker, and I wasn't even sick.

It was tough sitting there on the end of the bench, because the one thing I do have pride about—the one thing I have a big ego about—is playing. I don't want to just sit there. If I am on a team, I want to play and contribute. I wasn't contributing when the Little Fella took over. I learned that in business: you go with whom you love, and that is just a fact.

You go with whom you love.

One or two sportswriters were Lenny fans, so they said it was a good move. Some were on my side. It became a soap opera. I got sick of it. Everyday it was in the papers. Everyday it was on the radio. Cameras were at my house talking about it. It just became negative, and I knew I couldn't win.

THE UNTHINKABLE

On January 4, they told me that I had been traded to the Jazz. Two years after Bob Walsh told *Sports Illustrated* that they would have to trade the entire organization if they traded me, I was gone. Lenny pretended he was doing me a favor, playing the public relations game, saying that they were trading me so I could be closer to home.

It was very emotional for me. I had just built a house in Bellevue. We were getting ready to settle down . . . I thought forever. That song about me was about to come out. Two months prior, I was on TV every day—and then I was gone.

I was so upset that I left the game against Kansas City that night at halftime. I caught a flight the next day. It was really painful flying over the city, looking down. Tears came over my eyes, and I said, "I'm gone."

Slick with his son, Donald.
From the Donald Watts Collection

Afterwards, Lenny tried to make it sound as if we both wanted it. "This was a mutual understanding," Lenny told Greg Heberlein. "Slick and I had been talking all along. Everything was above board. Why should there be [negative] fan reaction? We made a deal. It's over. Why not let it die? Slick wanted the deal as much as anyone. Slick and I have the highest regard for each other. It wasn't a personality conflict."

Just as I said, Lenny is a real smoothie.

I once said that God made me a little slice of heaven, and he called it Seattle. My son, Donald, who was born here, stayed here. I never did claim New Orleans or Houston—where I later played—as home. To me, Seattle is still that little slice of heaven.

DOGGED

Later on, when Lenny wrote a book, there is a part about me, and he roasts me, boy—he talks about me like a dog. I guess I struck a nerve with him.

He said I couldn't shoot. He said I couldn't shoot free throws. He never said what I could do, though, like lead the league in steals and assists. He just brought up my free throw shooting, and he said nobody wanted me. He talked about the meeting, about how the people loved me, and how he wanted to make sure people weren't upset that he traded me.

John Johnson once said to me: "You must have got on Little Fella's mind."

No, Little Fella and I played against each other, and I did hack him a lot. I was a hacker. I was a little guy. I had to fight to survive. So, I used to fight and scratch him on the hand. He didn't ever like that. He would talk about me bad when I played against him. Then when he became the coach, I knew I was out.

Now when I see him, we hug each other. "Hey man, Slick, how you doing?" he says.

I show him the proper respect, just as I do with Big Bill. "Hey Coach, how you doing, Coach?"

He is Coach to me. Both of them are. They were my coaches, so I give them respect—that comes from being an old country boy.

From the Donald Watts Collection

PAYBACK

The first time I played Seattle after I was traded, man—I was juiced. New Orleans was Pistol's team, but this was my game. I was crazy in that game, I was everywhere.

It was exactly two months to the day after I had been traded, so it was still fresh on my mind. I wanted to make a statement to Lenny, but I also wanted to play well for all my fans back in Seattle.

I didn't start, but I played 32 minutes and had 24 points, eight rebounds, four assists. I even made nine of 11 free throws. We won, 113-104.

Lenny still wouldn't give me much credit. "Slick wasn't guarding anyone, as usual," Lenny told the *Seattle Times.* "He was just following the ball around, and we didn't make him pay."

Then I came back to Seattle two weeks later, and I was drained. It was all so emotional for me. Coming back, seeing my

From the Donald Watts Collection

From the Donald Watts Collection

family, seeing my friends, being where I used to play. I don't think anybody could have kept up the intensity that I had showed in New Orleans. It was just too much for any human.

I played okay. I had 16 points, four rebounds, and four assists, but I shot poorly, and we lost, 123-98.

From the Donald Watts Collection

FINALS RUN

After I was traded, the Sonics completed one of the best turn-arounds in sports history. They went from 5-17 to playing against the Washington Bullets for the NBA championship.

I think that so much stress from the previous seasons had been relieved, and the guys all came together and played.

For a while, our team was a soap opera. Russ was leaving. Hopkins was leaving. Lenny was coming in, hovering, and he had Hopkins backed into a corner because everybody knew Lenny was waiting to take over.

Once they fired Hopkins, all the stress went away. Everybody just relaxed and came to play. Then they traded me to New Orleans, and that was more stress gone because Hopkins had been my coach, and everybody knew we were tied together—and they also knew Lenny and I were on different pages.

It was like a bad marriage that finally comes together, and they began to find themselves and gel. These guys came together. No one should have gotten credit for it—everyone just relaxed. You become so stressed out at certain points in your life that there is no place to go but up—and they got that feeling.

At the end of that year, the team voted that I should get a playoff share. They could have voted me out, but they didn't. I got a little check from the team. Zollie sent it to me.

CHAMPIONSHIP

The next year, after getting a little taste of the Finals, the Sonics won the championship while I was playing in Houston in the last season of my NBA career.

I thought all these guys had been much like the Detroit Pistons team that won the title in 2004. All the players had been cast away by other teams.

Wally Walker had been with Portland; Dick Snyder was with Cleveland; Joe Hasset didn't play much; Marvin Webster had been given away a thousand times; Jack, nobody in the city wanted him when they drafted him; Fred, every year they were talking about trading him; Lonnie Shelton, they said his party life was better than Rodman's back in those days.

Really, if you gave somebody the opportunity, no one would admit putting this team together. Look at the names. Come on—this was a bunch of overachievers, and their time had come.

Just like my time came. I became "Slick Watts." I don't know why. If I was playing today, I might be just another player, but back then—it was my time. And it was those guys' time when they won that title.

People ask me, "Slick, how do you feel that you weren't on the '79 championship team?"

That wasn't my time. It was my time to be who I became a few years earlier. I don't know why it happened. Life is about timing, and it was their time. Nobody put those guys together thinking they would win a championship. Look at it. Think about it. It just happened—and I was happy for them. I still am.

CHAPTER 12

AFTER SEATTLE

IN RETROSPECT

If I had known then what I knew before I left, I would have hung out in Seattle. I don't care how badly they treated me; I would have stayed here.

Because I thought it was about the game—you get in practice, and I beat you out, or you beat me out. I take the ball from you, or you take the ball from me. I found out about the business side even more painfully.

You have to understand as a player, and as a person, if Joe Blow has the power, and his son wants a job that you want, his son is getting the job. He is going to try to give his son the advantage until he starts losing money. Some of these teams are losing money—and they still give their sons the job.

PETE'S TOWN

Elgin met me at the airport when I arrived in New Orleans, and I thought to myself, "Coach is meeting me at the airport. Damn, I'm in."

I couldn't have been more wrong. What Elgin said to me was: "I talked to Pete, and Pete doesn't mind you coming down here. But this is Pete's team." Elgin wanted me to know what Pete wanted me to know. Just like with Lenny in Seattle, there wasn't room for two superstars.

"Elgin, why did you bring me down here to sit me down?"

"Slick, you are not in Seattle. You have to wait your time and stay in your place."

"Elgin, I am from Mississippi. I understand that. You gave up a No. 1 draft pick to tell me that?"

What he was telling me was what I learned about top draft picks and politics. The players they bring in—I don't care how bad they are—they have to make it, or somebody is going to be fired.

I tell my son, I was tough because these jokers didn't want me there. As I said, the establishment doesn't want anybody rising from nowhere. Any time they saw me do something, they said, "Oh, that was Slick—he shouldn't be doing that, sit him down." If they send me home—ain't no big thing. Nobody is going to cry about it. However, if you send a top pick home, somebody is going to question you.

Elgin also told me he had rules and regulations for me. I was upset for a minute, but I think he was trying to tell me that the team was run by big business. I don't know if it was mafia or not—the word was that New Orleans was run by the small mafia. That's what they used to say. I don't know anything about that now. I was just a small-town boy who was traded into that situation, but that was the rumor.

Anyway, Elgin told me I had to roll with the punches and work with the system.

THE PISTOL

When I came down, Pete was cold, but he wasn't only cold to me. Pete was the man in New Orleans. I thought Spencer and all these guys had big egos and big issues about their lives.

In New Orleans, we all stayed on the third floor—Pete stayed on the first floor. That was in the days before the NBA made the rules about everybody getting their own room. We shared rooms, but Pete and Elgin had single rooms.

I was a dummy. I had led the league in steals and assists. I got used to men being men. At that point, I wasn't intimidated by anybody. I used to sit in Pete's seat on the bus and try to get me a room on the first floor.

Pete used to always sit on the bus in the last seat or the first seat. So I jumped in the first seat, and they said: "You can't sit there, that's Pete's seat."

Elgin used to say, "No, Slick, this is Pete's team."

FEUDING WITH PETE

The fans loved Pete because he was a great entertainer. Pete was like Isiah Thomas—a small basketball player who could dominate the ball. He was a popular, high-scoring guard. They say they brought me down there for security. Pete did many crazy things and was hurt often, so they wanted me there in case he got hurt, and because I could play defense well.

Pete reminded me of Bill Russell a little bit, too. It was all right for him to crack a joke on you, talk about you, talk about your head, talk about what you got on, but you didn't crack a joke back. He was a powerful personality. As long as the joke was on you, he was cool.

He would laugh with the group when he was delivering the punch line. The team had a policy that when the big boy said something, they all laughed at you because they didn't have enough guts to stand up to him. I was a guy who would punch you back, because I had been through all sorts of stuff in my life.

We got a little feud going. I would try to get a joke back on him if he tried to crack about my head, because he had that long-haired mop head, just like Pat Riley used to have.

When I said something back to him, he'd say: "Slick's trying to take over."

COACH PETE

Pete had so much power down there that he could dictate who played. I was rolling one night, Pete got Elgin's attention, pointed at me, and I was out of the game. I just sat my butt down because there was nothing I could do.

That's when Elgin told me, "Slick, you've just got to play by the rules."

Elgin was quiet as a coach. He called timeout and wasn't as intimidating as Russ and Hopkins were. He handled himself like Lenny Wilkens.

BORN AGAIN

At some point, Pete got religion. He didn't change in New Orleans. He changed in Boston. He changed, and he wrote his book.

Then when he saw me again, he hugged me, and talked to me, and he was warm. He had a Bible in his hand. It was almost as if he wanted us to forgive him for being the way he had been.

HOUSTON

After my less-than-stellar season in New Orleans—at least on the court, though I'll never forget staying in the Wilt Chamberlain suite at the Hyatt Regency—I got traded to Houston for a first-round draft pick before the start of the next season.

That is my one claim to fame, the thing that I like to brag about and point out. I came into this league as an undrafted free agent—passed over by every team in every round of the draft. Nobody knew who I was, and I was traded for not one, but two No. 1 draft picks.

Seattle traded me to New Orleans for a 1981 No. 1 that the team used to take Danny Vranes out of Utah. He played for the team for five seasons.

Then New Orleans traded me to the Rockets for a No. 1 pick that New Orleans used to take Danny Schayes. How's that for strange? Danny Vranes and Danny Schayes. Schayes played for the Jazz for two seasons, averaging 13 points and nine rebounds his final year there.

Anyway, Houston was a great experience in many ways. When Pete came back from his injury, I was playing well, but it was Pete's town. I wasn't taking over for Pete. The Jazz told me that Houston was interested in me because Mike Newlin broke his hand. Tom Nissalke and Del Harris wanted me down there.

Rick Barry was there, though, and I had to be careful with that situation. Rick was a point forward, and not only did he want to score, he wanted to make the play as well. So, I stepped aside and let Rick do his thing.

BEFRIENDING MURPH

When I first got to the Rockets, Calvin Murphy felt threatened. I understood. That is human nature. He thought I was coming to be The Man. At first we didn't get along; we didn't understand each other, and we had some battles—some premier battles.

We went after each other. It hurt both of us. He was hard, and I was hard. I was skinny, but I was hard. I thought he was the hardest body that I ever bumped. I started giving him some respect, too. Every time he touched me, he hurt me—and he said the same thing about me.

He soon found that, if he'd free himself on the wing, I wouldn't hesitate to pass it to him. So we became pretty good friends. I found out he was a nice guy. He found out I had a good heart.

We used to get on the bus and talk, and he would laugh and joke with me. He would tell me about how he liked fat women.

"A dog don't like no bone," he'd tell me, laughing. "A dog wants something with some meat on it. Nobody likes a bone. I want something with some meat on it."

BENCHED . . . AGAIN

We were doing pretty well that year—but still they called me in and said, "We are doing well, but Mike Newlin is off the injured list."

By this time, I knew the system. I had to stop playing. They just told me to be patient—again. They said when we got down by 15, be ready. I always had to be on the sidelines, warming up, staying ready in case somebody was kicking our butts.

So what I did, I turned into a fun guy. I started learning about the clubs because I knew I would not play very often.

I used to hang at a place called Elons. Real nice. Laid back. Gorgeous people. Backgammon. Beautiful limbos.

That was when I met Joe Morgan, the baseball player. We were the only two brothers in the place; so quite naturally, we started talking. Joe is an intelligent, good guy.

THE END

We had a good team—Rick, Murph, Rudy Tomjanovich, Mike Newlin, Big Mo. But we were disappointing in the playoffs, losing to Atlanta in two games and getting knocked out.

The next year, I came into training camp. Del Harris had replaced Tom Nissalke as the coach. And Del and I—we didn't get along. We weren't the best of buddies.

Del used to call me "Grasshopper," like the guy in the show *Kung Fu*. I had been called a ton of names my whole life, but having been in Seattle a few years, and being loved there, I had become sensitive about people calling me names. I didn't like being called Grasshopper.

One day, my son Donald got lost up in Seattle. He was living there with his mama. He was lost for four or five hours. I thought somebody had kidnapped him. Really, he just wandered out the door while his mom was upstairs. The police found him in Bellevue, but while he was lost, I had a lot on my mind because Donald is my heart.

Del called me Grasshopper that day, and I went off on him. I was ready to take him down. He was six foot five, but I was quick, and I was ready to go after him because I was mad. One time Big Mo elbowed me in practice, I grabbed his hands, and I took him down because my hands were strong. I was skinny, but I was in shape. I was ready to do the same thing to Del, and that's when I knew my time was over.

They told me if I could accept not playing unless they needed me, then I could come back. I was a competitor. What made me was my fire. They were asking me to extinguish my fire. So I said, "Okay, I'm gone."

I took the highest salary I ever took in my life, and I wasn't even playing. I was rich, and I wasn't even playing. The system had caught up with me. You have to learn from it. I didn't drive off a bridge and try to blame anybody. Like I say to my son, "Whatever happens in your life, you are responsible for it."

I don't care what it is—that's the way I live.

SHEATH THE PEN

They say the pen is mightier than the sword, but back then the telephone was more powerful. The telephone is more powerful then the pen, because word gets around. Jerry Colangelo called to see if Phoenix could use me, but he got word from Houston, and it was over for me. I went from a guy who would pick up a charge and hustle to a superstar. Houston told people that I wanted to be a superstar.

Then, for some reason, I moved up the ladder and was looked at as a franchise player. Because of my popularity, the NBA started looking at me differently. My agent called around and GMs started saying, "No, we have a franchise player already."

"Franchise player? I'm no franchise player. I pick up charges."

That's when I knew it was over for good.

GRAZIE

When I left the NBA, I played in Versace, Italy for six weeks. Fred Slaughter, a lawyer out of L.A., started representing me a little bit and found a job for me over there.

It took me 11 hours to get over there. They put me up in a place—a bad place . . . a real bad place. But I had a good time.

Bruce Seals was on the team, too. I played with Bruce in college for two years. Bruce was on that '78 team that went to the Finals, too. He didn't play much, but he was on it.

Anyway, Bruce was six foot eight, so he was in a nice place. He was all alone, so he told me to come and live with him.

Playing in Italy.
From the Donald Watts Collection

The party life was different there. These guys, they don't really hit on you, but they dance with you. Two guys would just come up and dance with you, and I don't go for that.

"No—no dance, no dance," I would tell them.

I learned a few words, a few pickup lines. It was fun—but at the same time, it was stressful because I wasn't paid much.

WHERE'S THE DOUGH?

I met a lady in Italy just before I met my second wife in 1978-79. Her dad owned Bally shoes—but he also owned my team. He didn't like to pay on time. I was dating his daughter, and I think he thought that was enough payment.

Every game I played, I did well and he kept saying to me, "You'll get your money. You keep playing hard."

So one day, a guy came to my door and said, "Your money, your money, count it."

It took me about five days to count it. I was impressed until I took it to the airport and found out what it was worth. That's when I found out that the exchange rate was 40 lira to the dollar.

I was paid about eight million lira. I thought I was rich because I had this big old sack of money. I took it to the airport to cash my money in because that was the only place I knew of that would exchange money. I thought I was going to be hit over the head carrying around this big old sack of lira.

It came out to about $2,400, and he owed me about $12,000 that month. I played a few more games, hoping he was going to pay me—but he never did.

ESCAPE

Bruce Seals and another kid who had played with the Milwaukee Bucks and I were playing on the same team, and we were winning. After we started winning, they started arguing, saying we had too many Americans on our team. You were only allowed two. So they had to let one of us go.

So I told Bruce and the other big boy, "I'm going to get out of here." The owner called me "hippy" because I was always smiling and happy. "You good hippy, you good hippy."

I told him: "This good hippy is getting his ass out of here."

What happened is, we played a game, we won, and they told the boy from Milwaukee he had to go home.

I told him, "No, don't leave, I'm getting out of here," but the team started watching me. They knew one of us was going to get out of there, but they wanted the boy from Milwaukee to leave.

I saw people start watching me. So one night, I got my rental car, got my bags, threw it in the car, drove to the airport, and left the car running out front of the airport and ran inside. I left the car running and got on the plane.

When the plane got to New York, they said, "Nobody get off the plane, we have a problem." I thought they were coming to get me because I left the car running in the middle of the street. They made us wait an hour and a half to get off. I almost went to the bathroom on myself I was so scared.

But what happened was the door locked on the plane and they couldn't get it open. When I touched ground in New York, I was the happiest person on the planet.

AND I THOUGHT NEW ORLEANS WAS BAD

There were just rumors the mafia was running the Jazz, but the guys are tough there in Italy. They do gamble on the games and the wins and losses. That's why they have the fights like the Pistons and Pacers. People throw stuff at you.

You could tell the games were fixed by the way they coached sometimes. Sometimes you played a ton of minutes, but sometimes you got 28, and you played only two minutes the next night. There was shady stuff happening there.

CHAPTER 13

TESTIMONIALS

BOB HOPKINS

"When I started recruiting Slick, I was working at Alcorn State. He was in high school at the time. His sister, who was at Alcorn, kept telling me: 'You don't know what you are missing.'

"The first time I saw him, they played a game in Vicksburg, Mississippi—he put on a dazzling show. I was a little surprised. After that, I was going to try to recruit him.

"However, what happened is, I went to Xavier, and he got away from me. When I tried to contact him, he was not around. Someone said he had gone to Grand View in Iowa. So, I kept trying to contact him, and when I finally did, I got him to come to Xavier. I brought him down there, and the rest is history.

"He was an outstanding ballplayer. Slick was always a person who was very confident. He liked to talk it up and get opponents all riled up. So I always had to try to cool him down a little bit so he didn't say things that they could put on the bulletin board."

"This one day, Slick was on the bus, and we were getting ready to go play a game. He ran off to go pick something up, and as he was coming back across the campus, I had the bus leave him. We were leaving at a certain time, and he wasn't there—so we left.

"And when we got up to Louisiana College, Slick was already there. He beat the bus there, and he had an outstanding game. With that kind of motivation, I wasn't going to keep him from playing. I believe he got a team manager to drive him up there.

"Said Slick: 'I was getting my pillow. My tailbone, man, it was hurting. So, I was going to get my pillow. That's why they called me 'Soft Booty.'

"Slick was probably one of the more outstanding individual defensive players the minute he came into the league. Even though he was small, he could play guys six foot five, six foot six, six foot seven. Most of them, the first thing they wanted to do was exploit him. So, they would take him down in the post, and he ended up getting steals and stuff. He would play behind the guy, and when they would catch it, he would come right around in front of the guy and strip him, and take it. He was very good at that.

"I don't really believe that he ever got all his due, being the kind of player in the league that he was. Red Auerbach always accused him of playing a zone. And yeah, he would leave his man and go help, but it didn't mean it was a zone. I mean, you could switch, you could leave your man and catch a guy reversing.

"Not from an offensive standpoint but a defensive one, Slick could have easily made the All-Star team. But there were so many good guards, and people often base stuff on points. Paul Silas was one of the first guys who made it on defense and rebounding."

CLIFFORD RAY

"Oh, we had a great time in Hawaii one time. Slick's wife, my girlfriend, and the two of us went over there; we were going to play in an All-Star game that Willie Norwood had.

"We went on this tour to go up to a place called 'Seven Second Falls.' We started out, and it was kind of nice until you got to this bamboo forest. Then you got by the waterfall, and the water was falling from so high up that it looked like it was raining all the time.

"In one little area, there was just all this mud from the rain. There was a lady who was in all white. I'll never forget this: Even before she went in, Slick said, 'Boy, this woman is in for some kind of hurting.'

"But you get to the point where you have gone too far to go back and too far not to finish. By the end, this lady got so muddy

Accepting a gift from another young fan.
From the Donald Watts Collection

that she finally just sat down and cried. Slick and I were just dying watching this lady. Slick is a funny guy. Just the things that he says, the way he sees life."

RALPH BARBIERI
(Author of "Slick Watts Towers Over Bill Russell")

"Back then, the late great Dick Schaap was the editor of *Sport* Magazine. Dick commissioned me to do many stories. I did a cover story on Bruce Jenner. I did the first cover story on Bill Walton. Yet, I can say unequivocally that the best time I ever had was the week I spent in Seattle doing the story on Slick.

"I understand that people put on shows for reporters. But I like to think that I am pretty discerning. Slick just seemed like one of the most real, sincere, and nicest people I ever met.

"First of all, Russell was a prick. The guy would not meet with me. I went to the University of San Francisco. I had flown up and spent a week in his town. The first day I was supposed to meet with him, he said he didn't have time—that I should come to his office the next day. So I went to his office the next day, and I explained that I was in town to do a story, and that I went to the same alma mater. He was standing ten feet away from me in his office, and he would not meet with me. His secretary apologized and said he was busy.

"I just remember Slick was immensely popular. Everywhere the guy went, people loved stopping and talking to him. Back then, the NBA required guys to do like two or three appearances a year. Slick did something like 300. When I was there, some lady asked him to come to her kid's birthday party—and he went.

"I remember Slick used to wear this jumpsuit with his name 'Slick' embroidered over the left breast pocket. Guys were going around in jump suits and shaving their heads, imitating Slick just to get girls."

Slick clowns around with a group of kids at a community event.
From the Donald Watts Collection

BOB BLACKBURN

"One of my favorite memories of Slick is that he became a very good tennis player in his post-basketball years. There was a time when I was a good tennis player, and I played with him back in the days when I was kind of even-up with him.

"This one time I got going with Slick, and I was about halfway near the net. And I put the ball in one corner, then I would bring it back and go to the other corner. Then I'd go back to the other corner. I did this about six or seven times.

"And Slick said, 'What the hell are you doing, Blackburn?'

"And I said, 'I'm just trying to see if you are as fast as I always said you were on the radio.' He was, too. He got every one of those balls.

"We gave him a lot of publicity, but I tell you what—he earned it. He was colorful. He was a guy who, when he was on the court . . . he never quit.

"One of the great memories is of the game against Detroit, when we were down by six, and he scored or helped score the next eight points. Bill Russell called timeout, and he called the final play for Fred Brown. Slick wouldn't give Fred the ball. He hit the final shot. Man, what a game that was!

"Bill Russell himself is a very free spirit—he still is. I think he respected Slick because Slick had that same free spirit in him. At times, though, I think he drove Bill nuts because of the gambles he made.

"Bill was a free spirit off the court, and Slick was a free spirit both on and off the court. Bill was not a free spirit on the court, necessarily. In his own way, he wanted the game to be played his way. From that standpoint, I am not sure he was a free spirit like Slick. If the guys didn't do it the way Bill wanted them to do it, he would lay into them."

WALT FRAZIER

"He and 'Downtown' Freddy Brown, they were always up for me. Man, it was very difficult playing against those guys. Especially out there, whenever we played in Seattle, they were always tough. He was one of the early guys who were small but tenacious. He created a lot of havoc, getting into the paint. He was just relentless, man, just relentless."

RUDY TOMJANOVICH

"I just thought the guy was a pretty doggone good player. Being bald at the time was something of a novelty, but I just thought the guy could play, and I was glad that he was on our team for a while.

"We were shooters then, so we were all happy to have a guy who loved getting an assist. I mean, are you kidding? We were all happy to see him. And I have to say, the point guards on that team were always getting crap from the other four guys to pass to them. I thought he was a pretty darn good player. And I just remember he was a character."

JACK SIKMA

"I was sitting down getting ready for my first game in the pros. And Slick was a locker or two down. We had vitamin packs, and one of the vitamins in the pack was the little Vitamin E tablet with the gel in the middle.

"So I looked down and watched Slick bite the tip off the Vitamin E, squeeze it into his hand, and put it on his head so he could shine up his head. Then the headband went on and here we go.

"I looked around the room. I don't remember who it was, but somebody clued me in what the whole deal was with the Vitamin E tablet. That's what he used to shine up his head. He had to be ready for his fans.

"Slick penetrated all the time, so we did meet in the middle quite a bit in practice. I do remember one time Hoppy said, 'Slick, why do you continue to go in the middle?' I mean, certainly I wasn't the only big guy in there hitting Slick.

"And Slick turned to Hoppy and said, 'Man, I'm working on my game.'

"And Hoppy told him, 'Well, Slick, there's a few other guys in the gym. We can't all stand around and watch you go in the middle and get knocked down.'"

TALVIN SKINNER

"Slick and I played each other in college. He played at Xavier, and I played at Maryland-Eastern Shore. So, we first played each other in a tournament in Kansas City. I remember when I first played him in college—I couldn't believe it. He had this bald head, and he just looked weird. Head band, bald head—back then everybody had afros.

"Seattle was his city. Literally, it was his city. When you said Seattle, you had to say Slick Watts. There was just something about him. Even now, when you see him, people still love him. He's a special individual, he really is. Once you get to know him and find out what he is about, you find that he'd do anything for you.

"Playing with Slick is like playing with Determination and Will. Every minute, he is going to give it everything he has. He's just fun to be around. Any time you lead the league in steals and assists, that is pretty special. That is not something that you just do. Only three guys in the history of the league have done it, and one (John Stockton) will be in the Hall of Fame. He's just one of those guys who, any time you stepped on the court with him, you felt like you had a chance to win."

BOB LANIER

"I don't think Slick ever got enough credit for what he did both on and off the floor. Guys like me who knew him and played against him and competed against him, we had a lot of respect for him. I personally have a lot of respect for him. He understood the game and knew how to play it on both ends of the floor.

"We used to hook up because when I was in town he used to take me out to eat. I would get in that tiny Volkswagen and feel like a sardine. They used to have to pry me out. I couldn't do it anymore. That was when I had better knees.

"When he went into Sundays, man—he was like an icon in Sundays. So being with Slick, you just kind of felt as if you were bigger than life. He was just a good dude, and that's why we hung out with him."

Celebrate the Heroes of Basketball
in These Other Releases from Sports Publishing!